Complete *by the* Master's Touch

To Tim,
May God bless
you as you read
Love Your Friend,
to you! John

Complete *by the*
Master's Touch

Dr. John A. Catanzaro

Pleasant Word
A Division of WINEPRESS PUBLISHING

Printed in the United States of America

Packaged by Pleasant Word, a division of WinePress Publishing, PO Box 428, Enumclaw, WA 98022. The views expressed or implied in this work do not necessarily reflect those of Pleasant Word, a division of WinePress Publishing. Ultimate design, content, and editorial accuracy of this work are the responsibilities of the author.

Unless otherwise noted, all Scriptures are taken from the King James Version of the Bible.

Scripture references marked NKJV are taken from the New King James Version, © 1979, 1980, 1982 by Thomas Nelson, Inc., Publishers. Used by permission.

Scripture references marked NASB are taken from the New American Standard Bible, © 1960, 1963, 1968, 1971, 1972, 1973, 1975, 1977 by The Lockman Foundation. Used by permission.

ISBN 1-4141-0115-5
Library of Congress Catalog Card Number: 2004100345

Dedication

To Anna, my life companion and friend, and to all my children—God has taught me much through your lives. To my Lord Jesus, who still heals the sick and inspired this work, may the miracle and blessing of healing come to those who read the accounts contained in the Scripture and a greater dimension of hope, faith, and trust in the Master Healer, our Lord Jesus Christ, be experienced.

I want to give special thanks to my editor, Judith Perry. The Holy Spirit has directed the manuscript to you and through your gifted work accented it with an inspirational flow that the reader can embrace.

I also want to give special thanks to Athena, David, Lisa, and Tammy at Pleasant Word for sensitivity to God's direction in producing the work from cover to cover.

Table of Contents

Introduction

Healing is often defined incompletely. It is a word that often implies relief from physical and emotional suffering. However, it is so much more than that. Healing describes the process of being made well in an area that once was wrought with pain, grief, deep wounds, and other elements of the human experience that threaten to steal away the essence of life. Biblical accounts of Jesus' ministry of healing tell us that the healings Jesus performed were supernatural. God touched these people in ways not visible to others. He touched them in secret places only He can reach.

We need the touch of God today. We are faced with uncertainty that permeates our human experience. We are living in the "Post-Christian era," and the return of our Lord is close at hand. The greatest healing any of us can experience is to accept and follow Jesus as Lord and Master. This is a personal decision made by faith. Billy Graham, God's servant and messenger, delivers this vital message. He urges humanity to accept the message of salvation and holiness in Jesus Christ.

President George W. Bush tells of a healing experience that pointed him to a personal faith in Jesus Christ. He was at a crucial time of spiritual need when he and Billy Graham discussed the meaning of a personal decision for Jesus. Dr. Graham asked this question, "Are you right with God?" The President states that a personal faith is "a charge to keep," and he now shares his personal faith with the world. This was the beginning of the Lord's healing in George Bush's life—a healing that sets the heart free from the wounds of the past. When we accept this free gift we are covered with forgiveness, holiness, and love of Jesus.

As we embrace this message and begin to live our personal faith, we are at the beginning point of healing. The wounds and pains of the past can be transformed into peace and joy with the Master's touch. Personal faith in Jesus opens the way to knowing the purpose of life, and God's plan for us begins to unfold. Nothing escapes His eye. He knows the pain, affliction, loneliness, challenge, and continual stress of life.

Jesus was tested and tried and knows grief, sorrow, and loss. But He also knows the joy of living, and we are urged in the New Testament to not be downtrodden for He has overcome the world that we may have abundant joy in the midst of trouble. He provides the power we need for living holy in a troubled time.

Jesus still reaches out to us through the Holy Spirit today, healing the sick and brokenhearted. My friend, if you are lonely, sick, tired of living, hopeless, and feel that there is no purpose for your life, then this book is for you. You are special to God, and your life has a great purpose. Jesus wants to heal you, and He wants to bring purpose to your life. Say yes to God. His healing will bring you all of this—and more!

CHAPTER ONE

Jesus Still Heals the Sick

"Bless the Lord O my soul and forget not all his benefits: who forgiveth all thine iniquities; who healeth all thy diseases"
(Psalm 103:2–3)

The healing ministry of Jesus comprised some amazing life miracles. The majority of Jesus' ministry was one of healing the sick. This healing was not just a physical experience alone. He demonstrated the healing power of God for conditions that affect the human psyche and spirit. Jesus always demonstrated, through the healing of people, the object lessons of God.

Our generation is in great need of the Great Physician to heal our diseases. However, we are free and independent agents while sojourning on this planet; God does not intrude in our lives. He gives us the ability to choose our paths with the hope that we would not forget Him. Human nature tends to forget God and seek earthly pleasures instead of worshipping the God who has the power over life and death.

As we explore the healing ministry of Jesus, we will see that God, through Jesus, was the compassionate Friend who understood human need and lovingly and graciously met those needs. Jesus was not superficial. He was able to relate to every human on every age level.

When Jesus healed the sick He demonstrated the newness of life and the precious blessings of it. His words "come and see," "go and tell," "rise up and walk," "receive thy sight," "thy faith hath made thee whole," "who touched me," "be thou cleansed" and "be healed" demonstrate the miracle of healing. One of the greatest disputes within the Christian church is that the miracles of divine healing do not pertain to the church of the Twenty-first Century. This miracle of healing belonged to the apostolic age and is no longer active in the church today. However, the New Testament affirms with Jesus that He was going to send the Helper and the Comforter to guide us into all truth. The Comforter, Helper, and Guide is the Holy Spirit of God; He is able to work the miracle of healing today just as Jesus did over two thousand years ago.

Miracle healing has a negative reputation today due to individuals who abuse their position and falsely proclaim the power of God. These so-called godly healers make a show of healing as if they are playing stage tricks. Healing does exist, but it continues to be directed and administrated by God for those He touches and makes whole. There is a simple formula that mankind must recognize: God's existence represents power, authority, omnipotence, and omniscience. Man's part of the formula should be faith, submission, and obedience. Man *alone* is not vested with the authority, power, and presence to heal man. It is *always* God who works the miracle—and man merely experiences it.

The healing miracles repeatedly performed by Jesus in the New Testament were motivated and brought about by His compassion and empathy of human need. Jesus penetrated the deepest soul and spirit maladies and provided *complete* healing. This healing was not a public spectacle for the world to see; it was for the benefit of man. It was a testimony of the power of God over all the earth. Jesus never intended to profit from the misfortunes and sufferings of man or to elevate himself to a higher station of life. Jesus did not receive nor expect material profit while ministering to the needs of others.

Jesus fed the five thousand from a poor boy's lunch. He restored sight by using clay fashioned by His own hands—His plan was so simple that the writing in the sand while a woman stood scorned liberated the woman and defused the accusing crowd. A great miracle happened that day as the woman was forgiven and the Prince of Peace gave peace to her. No coins were exchanged for these life-changing events. Jesus had nowhere to lay His head, and He often stood in the gap for a faithless generation.

Jesus still stands in the gap to intercede for you and me and to protect us today. In this book I will outline the true and complete healing that Jesus exercised while on earth and still exercises today through the presence of the Holy Spirit. My prayer is that this book will provide clear direction and understanding of healing and its effect on human sickness and that God will demonstrate greater lessons through the acceptance of His healing. The personal journey of faith in Jesus and His ability to heal teaches us what it means to submit to God's unfailing presence and love. It shows us His gentleness during times of brokenness and his continual flowing rivers of peace during times of trouble. The secret of the Lord rests in His power to heal the very core of man.

CHAPTER TWO

The Journey Toward Healing

The road is hard, the journey swift. As we travel towards the grave.

This body will return to dust, but what of the soul to save?
(Selected)

But those things which proceed out of the mouth come forth from the heart; and they defile the man. For out of the heart proceed evil thoughts, murders, adulteries, fornications, thefts, false witness, blasphemies: These are the things which defile a man: but to eat with unwashen hands defileth not a man.
(Matthew 15:18–20)

What Are the Events in Life that Make Us Sick?

The experiences of life that sicken the heart and sadden the spirit are what Jesus made reference to on many occasions during His healing ministry. Identifying those experiences is the beginning point of our journey toward healing. Jesus advocated that it is not the things around us that trouble our hearts; it is the events within our hearts that cause us trouble. Listed below are some of the events of the heart that sadden the soul and trouble the spirit.

1. **Loss of Touch with God**
    An individual's relationship with God determines how long sickness and sadness remain in the heart and spirit. God is not cruel and indifferent. How can we possibly escape the trouble and afflictions that this present world has to offer without God? It was by disobedience and direct rejection of God that sickness and sadness were introduced. You can read this in the first book of the Bible and learn about the origins of suffering. With God, there is the assurance of peace, justice, mercy, forgiveness, and acceptance. All of us, being the creation of God, have the opportunity to know God and trust God, but few embrace the opportunity and make it a life commitment. Being out of touch with God is a lonely place to be. In contrast, union and friendship with God is the heart's warm and secure home.

2. **Loss of Self-respect, Love, and Acceptance**
    It is difficult to have a firm grip on self-respect without God. Life does not always offer the best opportunities, and undesirable experiences in childhood and early adult life may negatively affect how one will view oneself. For example, growing up with only one or no parents, living in danger and in poor living conditions, growing up unloved, having poor role models of how to properly love others, emphasis on greed and material possessions rather than concern for the wellbeing of others, or living with spiritual, physical, emotional, or sexual abuse will adversely affect one's self image.

3. Loss of Physical Health

Sometimes we ignore the things that matter most. Many instances in the New Testament demonstrate how disconnected people can be to the suffering of others. I often think of the man who was brought down to the Pool of Siloam; he suffered for years from his physical infirmity—blindness—but the majority of the people who were present saw him every day and had no idea the suffering this man experienced.

> *And as Jesus passed by, he saw a man which was blind from his birth. And his disciples asked him, saying, Master, who did sin, this man, or his parents, that he was born blind? Jesus answered, Neither hath this man sinned, nor his parents: but that the works of God should be made manifest in him. I must work the works of him that sent me, while it is day: the night cometh, when no man can work. As long as I am in the world, I am the light of the world. When he had thus spoken, he spat on the ground, and made clay of the spittle, and he anointed the eyes of the blind man with the clay, And said unto him, Go, wash in the pool of Siloam, (which is by interpretation, Sent.) He went his way therefore, and washed, and came seeing.*
>
> (John 9:1–7)

Disconnecting from pain and suffering is common. When Job experienced the cruelty of his supposed three friends, what they demonstrated by their attitude was disconnection from Job's pain. The reality of traumatic and tragic suffering was not apparent to them. How could this happen to a man who was well respected and loved by God? It was questionable and suspicious of some kind of disobedience. The three friends of Job were demonstrating their unwillingness to understand the purpose of Job's suffering. They evaluated the situation through eyes with human limitation, wanting to ignore the life lessons of pain and suffering. A closer union with God and a greater sensitivity to what really matters in life is learned through hard times. Pain and suffering are reminders of the need to be constantly cared for and nourished by God. It is also a reminder that it's not about me; it's about God and His desire and purpose for me. It's about God's plan for me. In Job's and the blind man's experiences, the immediate response of those watching was that the suffering was caused by sin. In both cases God demonstrated His healing work. The blind man came away seeing by following the instructions given to him by Jesus. Job was blessed and restored in spite of his friends accusations. In fact, if not for Job's prayers for these three ungrateful, cruel individuals, they would have been taken out by God. Job prayed and trusted God, and he didn't allow bitterness or anger to spoil his view of God. Read the complete account of Job's life in the book of Job in the Old Testament.

Jesus understood the anguish of the blind man's soul and spirit as He understands the hurts, wounds, and maladies of all of His children. The blind man was set free and completely healed. This can be our experience with God.

Where Healing Begins

Then shall thy light break forth as the morning and thine health shall spring forth speedily and thy righteousness shall go before thee; the glory of the Lord shall be thy rearward . . . . And the Lord shall guide thee continually, and shall satisfy thy soul in drought, and make fat thy bones; and thou shall be like a watered garden, and like a spring of water, whose waters fail not. And they that shall be of thee shall build the old waste places; thou shalt raise up the foundations of many generations; and thou shall be called, the repairer of the breech. The restorer of paths to dwell in.

(Isaiah 58: 8, 11–12)

- **Understanding the Concept**
  Understanding the concept of healing is the starting point of the journey toward healing. Healing is a process that is

orchestrated by God and experienced by mankind. It can occur over time or as a miraculous, instantaneous work. Miracle healing is as prevalent today as it was for the apostolic age. It is a promise of God as outlined in the above portion of Scripture. There are several nuggets of truth revealed. This passage talks about light as the morning, health springing forth quickly, righteousness going before to guide, the glory of the Lord following wherever one moves, the continual guidance of the Lord, the satisfaction of the soul during the dry times, the fattening of the bones which is a symbol of prosperity, as a watered garden flourishing and full of life, as a spring of water—a continuous supply that never fails. Those who follow shall build the old waste places, new generations will be raised with this new standard of God, great repairs will be made and great restoration will take place. What a tremendous promise of God!

There are many avenues an individual can take to experience true healing. Often, it is not any one isolated event that we can put our finger on that offers such healing. However, there is one single truth that all can affirm—this being that healing begins on a personal level. I have observed in many individuals this single truth, and I have seen different dimensions of healing through their journeys. Individuals who are experiencing suffering in their physical, emotional, and spiritual health will often gravitate to resources that offer some explanation for the purposes of suffering. Such suffering often allows for deep reflection on what it means to live in the moment.

Pain and suffering can shape a new creativity and a compassionate love, replacing the most common mind ailments of depression and self-pity. God teaches us to focus on the eternally weighted things in life. Suddenly, we realize that there are people around us who are suffering, and for some strange reason we find a new comfort in the fact that suffering is not an isolated event. Then we try to learn the meaning of such suffering and begin to realize that there is a transformation occurring. It is a vital transformation, allowing each of us to realize, *I'm not here for myself. I'm here for God and His service, and that service is to love and serve Him with all I have and to love my neighbor with His love and demonstrate it by my actions. It is about taking personal responsibility for my actions and changing my old, self-centered patterns.*

It is often physical suffering that prompts deeper attention to the central core of life. There are essential points to ponder that move an individual toward liberation of soul and spirit, even when encountering physical suffering. Some of these are:

Why am I here?

What purpose does my life serve?

What is the mission God has for me?

How should I worship God?

How do I love and accept myself and others in God's way?

How should I love my spouse, children, and family members?

What does it mean to completely surrender to God?

What is my Christian duty and obligation?

What does it mean to be a good citizen?

How do I resist the darkness of this world?

The answers to these questions are found when a concentrated focus of growth is made in the human spirit. God communicates His answers to these questions over the course of a lifetime. Do you want all of these answers now? Of course you do. We want it all now. Would the answers be cemented into our innermost core and then put into practice if we had all of the answers instantly? Probably not. A textbook approach to life sometimes sounds good, but it is totally unrealistic. *Prepare us Lord, for the true miracle of healing. Help us come to a complete surrender to You and willingness to do anything You command.*

- **We Are in the Age of Miracles**
  The best defense against false healing is the true miracle of healing. In our society today there are many false assurances of healing and completeness apart from God. These ideologies emphasize body and mind interaction, and they usually don't clearly define the importance of the unity of body, soul, and spirit in light of total dependence upon divine sustenance. This is the result of an incomplete understanding of the interaction of the spirit, soul, and body the way God intended. God's foundational perspective of healing is demonstrated with intensity and power because of His presence. The great pioneers of faith found in the Bible and through the history of the Christian church set in motion the continuance of the gift of healing. Although this miracle is alive today, it is craftily hidden by the adversarial counterfeits. It is the human element that often obstructs the healing forces of God. The focus shifts to what gives immediate relief. Today we see a shift from a dependence upon medication to fix the problems that afflict the spirit or soul to a therapy or meditative force that gives a façade of pseudo-emotional and pseudo-spiritual euphoria. The use of medication and therapy for troubling ailments that affect the soul and spirit is the first approach in care. However, these medications and therapies often fail,

resulting in the realization that there are no miracle medicines that remedy the pain encountered in our souls and spirits. It is the world's way to deny the existence of the deepest aspects of life that should be given close attention because to give attention to our pain may spark some conviction and obligation that we don't want to face.

What is needed is healing from the *inside out*. Most healing systems being practiced today focus on healing from the *outside in*. The Bible tells us that the things that trouble our lives are housed on the *inside*. The *outside in* concept of healing offers coping strategies that focus on the externals of an individual that is expected to in some way affect how interaction between self, others, and the world environment should occur.

In today's society, cause and effect experimentation that is based upon individual philosophical belief rather than on biblical principle is the norm. However, it is contrary to God's intention. See the following table.

Inside Out (God-centered vertical healing)	Outside In (Human-centered horizontal healing)
• Based on the unchangeable principles of God • Origin is from omnipotent Creator • A free gift to all who accept • Based on truth (consistent)	• Focused on cause and effect • Evolutionary, philosophically based system • Seeks global and cultural acceptance • Pragmatic (whatever works is true)

- **Our Healing Is Our Need**
  In our need for the healing touch of the Master, we must trust that our need for healing is acknowledged by God. When we exercise faith and trust there may be some delays in seeing God's hand, but there are no failures. Healing is not always instantaneous. One reason may be because God's purpose needs to be revealed. A demonstration of growth in personal faith, trust, and total surrender could be what God is seeking in an individual's life. Sickness may allow the opportunity for a demonstration of God's grace, power, and divine comfort and care. Some sicknesses are experienced because of poor moral choices. Some sicknesses end in death. These are mysteries of God that I'm sure will be revealed when we see Him in glory.

- **We Need to See a Living Christ**
  Every generation needs the living Christ, and every community seeks the signs of healing to confirm the promises found in the Word. Hebrews 2:4: "God bears witness, both with signs and wonders. And gifts of the Holy Ghost, according to His own will." Jesus did not say, *I will* be with you always. He said *I am.* His standard does not change. It is not simply healing that is needed, but the power to be ready to serve God completely and without reservation. The gift of healing is free, but it requires the offering of a life of complete surrender to God and the promise that *I am* will be the source of all comfort and care.

- **The Great Physician Heals**
  In Matthew 8:16 Jesus healed the multitude. He healed all those who had need, and He did it on the Sabbath—much to the disapproval of His critics. Through this He proved

that healing was not of a secular nature, nor is it apart from the administrative work of God. Healing is a holy and sacred work of God that is consistent with His higher purpose for man. This healing offered salvation of the soul and restoration for the higher purpose of renewal and regeneration of the spirit.

The Bible mentions few doctors, and when it does their results are usually discouraging. As a matter of fact, Luke left the practice of medicine to become an evangelist and accompany the Apostle Paul in his travels. He observed more miracles through the power of the Holy Spirit than he had opportunity to administer medicine. This doesn't mean there is no use for physicians. It simply means that there is need for a physician who allows the supernatural force of God to work the miracle and is willing to be the vehicle used to facilitate this healing power. This requires the expenditure of soul and spiritual energy and greater faith, trust, prayer, and commitment to God.

- **Healing Requires Sympathetic Interaction**
  The individual who experiences illness usually becomes aware of the deeper significance and purpose of life. An individual who administers healing must first understand the needs of those who suffer. Second, he or she must feel sympathy regarding the pain of the experience. Finally, the individual must be willing to offer solutions that often require soul and spirit expenditure that are similar to what Jesus experienced when He healed the woman with the bleeding disorder.

Jesus said *"Who touched me?"* He felt the need of those who experienced anguish of spirit and soul, and He met the need. *"That it might be fulfilled which was spoken by Esaias the prophet, saying, Himself took our infirmities, and bare our sicknesses"* (Matthew 8:17).

Charles Spurgeon Gives a Sympathetic Account of What It Is Like to Administer the Gift of Healing

First, he bore our sicknesses by intense sympathy. When Christ looked at all those sick people, he did, as it were, take all their sicknesses upon himself. You know what I mean. If you talk with a person who is very ill, and you feel for him, you seem to lay his pains upon yourself, and then you have power to comfort him. When I am seeing troubled people, I enter into one sorrowful case after another till I am more sad than any of them. I try as far as I can to have fellowship with the case of each one, in order to be able to speak a word of comfort to him; and I can say, from personal experience, that I know of nothing that wears the soul down so fast as the outflow of sincere sympathy with the sorrowing, desponding, depressed ones. I have sometimes been the means in God's hand of helping a man who suffered with a desponding spirit; but the help I have rendered has cost me dearly. Hours after, I have been myself depressed, and I have felt an inability to shake it off. You and I have not a thousandth part of the sympathy that was in Christ. He sympathized with all the aggregate of human woe, and so sympathized that he made his heart a great reservoir into which all streams of grief poured themselves. My Master is just the same now. Though he is in heaven, he is just as tender as he was on earth." Healing is a journey involving our spirit and soul; without their involvement, the body cannot heal.[1]

Sympathy vs. Empathy

Jesus demonstrated sympathy throughout His healing ministry. We often hear that we are to empathize when we see suffering and affliction. Empathy reflects a certain disconnection from the deep sense of burden that one suffers. There is no identification and offering of compassion to an individual who is suffering. Sympathy, on the other hand, is a compassionate burden-sharing and a harmonious expression of care to the burdened and downhearted. Sympathy is a Bible-based expression of compassion. An example of sympathy is Jesus being moved with compassion toward the crowds and offering the hope of healing. An example of empathy is seeing a suffering individual and saying in a disconnected fashion: "I'm sorry that you are going through such suffering, and I'll pray for you." Great words, but that is all. There is a total disconnection, and the burdened individual knows it. It is easier to say "I will pray for you" than it is to say "I will share your burden." Saying you will share a burden is not the same as actually sharing it. It is better to keep silent than to offer words that are completely disconnected. If you are not willing to be there to share the burden with sympathy and compassion, your words mean nothing. Sympathy is what Jesus demonstrated when He met the needs of people.

Trust or Worry?

"Ask, and it shall be given you; seek and ye shall find; knock and it shall be opened unto you."

(Luke 11:9)

We have all heard the saying, "To err is human," and all humans have fallen into the category of *to err*. Francis of Assisi recognized many centuries ago that there was the natural tendency within him to be overly concerned about his selfish ambition in life. On one occasion his heart was set on defending his province in order to be top dog and find favor with Roman Church authorities. He felt this was a good pursuit because he stood firm to defend God and country. At that time, Francis was busy with his earthly endeavors but then was contacted by the highest Authority known to all of creation. These simple words from God came to Francis: "Why give service to the servant? You can serve the Master alone."

Immediately Francis knew that Jesus was calling him to service; he left his fishing net behind and became a fisher of men. Similar stories can be found in the history of the Christian church. What did Francis learn? He learned to be totally dependent upon his Creator for everything. His anxiety about life was converted into an assurance that cannot be known apart from God. This is reflected in his simple prayer:

Lord, make me an instrument of your peace. Where there is hatred, let me sow love. Where there is injury, pardon. Where there is discord, unity. Where there is doubt, faith. Where there is error, truth. Where there is despair, hope. Where there is sadness, joy. Where there is darkness, light. O Divine Master, grant that I may not so much seek to be consoled as to console; to be understood, as to understand. to be loved, as to love. For it is in giving that we receive. It is in pardoning that we are pardoned. It is in dying that we are born to eternal life.

What Can I Do with My Worry?

Worry is paralyzing, and it is experienced by countless numbers of people every day. Worry negatively affects health and is linked to panic disorders and uncontrollable emotions. It can cause illnesses such as cancer and contributes to high blood pressure and heart disease. It can also cause extreme fatigue and general loss of health. Many heart attacks, strokes, and chronic illnesses are caused by worry. There is never a shortage of things for us to worry about. Some of the more common worries include death, loss, health, finances, relationships, and the future.

The following comparisons have allowed me to convert worry into manageable concerns of life. It is essential to understand the origins, destinations, and foundational aspects of life experiences. Maybe the following comparison chart will be of help to you.

Heaven-Bound	Earth-Bound
• Vertical Thinking (God centered)	• Horizontal Thinking (Human centered)
• Faith	• Unbelief
• Trust	• Worry
• Priorities (thinks of others)	• Self-ambition (no room for others)
• Action (purpose in life)	• Inaction (Reactions to senseless situation ethics)

Ephesians 4:10 helps define the larger purpose of life: *"He that descended is the same also that ascended up far above all the heavens that he might fill all things."* When our focus is on things that are earth-bound we are living life in a descent pattern. We are bound by horizontal thinking that allows us to see things from the perspective of man rather than God. Vertical thinking allows us to look to the Divine Creator and yields eternal value that cannot be measured in earthly terms. The earth-bound scenario is confining and erects walls of defense and localities (living from situation to situation) that lock us in a box. There seems to be a false sense of security that accompanies this thinking. I call it *fear*. It could be the fear of losing approval of authority figures, friends, co-workers, thereby losing self worth. The typical thinking here is to not rock the boat and just put up with the dysfunction and disturbance. In other words, there is a huge tree blocking the road and there is no way around it, but we will just pretend it isn't there.

Fear, the Root of All Anxiety

The Bible says throughout the Old and New Testaments to *"fear not."* Recent findings reveal that anxieties can become strongly etched into the brain, and researchers are trying to discover ways to erase them. This is not humanly possible short of removing the portion of the brain that stores fear. There are no perfect medications that will erase fear entirely either. There are no new genetically-engineered substances to stop fear. In a recent article in *Scientific American Mind* the area said to be the most active region of the brain in cases of fear and anxiety is the amygdala, just below the temporal lobe. When researchers stimulated the area electrically, the levels of the hormone cortisol increased. I discuss cortisol and its involvement in the stress reaction in some detail later on. It is said that this portion of the brain can become scarred from intense emotional experiences that produce fear and anxiety.[2] Fear is a stressor of the brain that can cause irreversible damage.

Fear and worry are partners in crippling our trust and faith. There is a risk associated with shedding this horizontal, box-like thinking and becoming a vertical out-of-the-box thinker. You may have to develop new friendships, change employment, and take new action in how you communicate, but you will attain a new freedom. The changes that come about by this process will produce a new sense of confidence. Here are some examples:

1. Vertical Thinking: Putting into practice a new model of communication based upon vertical thinking. This is seeing God's higher purpose in your life. He has already given you the resources. He is waiting for you to ask and implement them.

2. Faith: Faith is the realization that God will and has performed all that He has promised. This will continue to become evident throughout human existence. This new communication is based upon knowing that all that is contained within your life-experience will work out for the good of all involved, even though the fruit of such action is not presently apparent.

3. Trust: Probably the biggest challenge to put into practice. Trust is the stabilizing element.

4. Priorities: Having a sense of service. This is not self-centered focus but rather a broader vision that includes benevolence and humanitarian action. In the long run this yields a lasting work of posterity. It is a continuous, selfless focus. It may seem that your labor is obscure. However, there is a light that rises from obscurity. Abraham Lincoln is a prime example of this. He was born in an obscure place and suffered many defeats before becoming president of the United States. This is a common story of most men and women who achieve great things. If you were to ask them for a list of characteristics that contributed to their greatness, they may tell you the following: ability to overcome obstacles, take action on matters that are within their control, and developing a strong trust in God.

5. Surrender: It is necessary to completely surrender to God and His plan. Surrender is not an act of resignation; it is an act of obedience. We are not giving up; we are submitting to His purpose and plan.

6. Action: Bring your vulnerabilities to the One who has the power to do something about them. He will give you the insight and confidence to do something about the things that touch your life. This is much different than reacting and moving from crisis situation to crisis situation. I know a person who currently has a job in crisis management. His responsibilities are to identify a crisis and provide strategies to resolve the crisis. I asked this person if any long-lasting resolves are practiced and he replied there really were none. Bandages cover the problem, but they don't address the core of the problem.

Moving from situation to situation by reacting instead of acting leads to a chaos. If we ask, God will give us a course of action, and if there is not an immediate action available to be taken, we must wait and not force the door open. The door may not be opened until we meet Jesus, and we must be willing to let it go until then if need be. This is a hard life lesson, but it beats repeatedly hitting your thumb with a hammer. My father-in-law told me that he learned as a carpenter that no matter how many times you hit your thumb with the hammer, it hurts every time. Some of his fellow carpenters said that if you hit your thumb once it becomes so numb that when you hit it the second time you don't feel it. I think it's best not to hit your thumb in the first place, and if you do, it's best to try not to do it again.

Some Helpful Hints in Overcoming Worry

1. **If you must worry, develop a worry list.** Identify the things you worry about and generate a list outlining specifics about each. When you see it plainly in front of you, you will realize the depth of your worries. Here is a sample worry list.

   > **Things I Am Worried About:**
   > Health of a loved one
   > My job or business
   > Finances
   > Challenging friendships
   > Future goals
   > Family relationships
   > Church relationships

2. **Develop a prayer list.** Convert the worry list into active prayer. Make your requests known to the God who can do

something about them. Here is a sample prayer list developed from the worry list.

- Provide healing of body, soul, and spirit of this loved one and help me to be a source of encouragement, service, and love.
- Help me to be a stabilizing influence in the job or business that I am currently in. Lead me into Your purpose and ministry for my life and help me, above all, to model the character of Jesus in my current experience and in future opportunities.
- I realize that Your resources are abundant. Teach me responsible ways to manage the resources You have entrusted to me. Help me be the good steward You desire me to be.
- My heart aches because of friends I have lost for whatever reasons. Help me to be open to the areas I need to change to mend friendships. I forgive those who have wronged me and maintain false perceptions.
- Guide me in future opportunities. Help me trust my future to You. My future is beyond my control. Help me rely on the grace and prudence You provide each day. Help me to be the salt of the earth and the light of the world today, for tomorrow has enough troubles.
- I ask You, O Lord, to intervene on delicate family matters. I ask You to rescue and bring each member of my family who does not know You to a personal commitment to You. Speak to them in a way that they can understand through the guidance of the Holy Spirit. May Jesus become their personal Guide and Friend.

- I ask You, O Lord, to intervene in complicated matters within the church. The church is Your ultimate concern, and I acknowledge that Your grace and guidance is sufficient. Help me take action in matters that You give me liberty in, and to leave with You particulars that only You can change. Help me to rise above the conflict and obstacles to achieve Your purposes.

3. **While you're at it, develop an action list.** Developing an action list takes paralyzing anxiety and fear and converts it to a manageable concern for the responsibilities of life. Here is a sample action list. This action list provides strategy for victory in God's ability and power to solve complex issues that challenge us.

   - Health needs: Identify the needs and appropriately provide for those needs with sensitivity and balance.
   - Develop effective communication strategies and become a person of influence. Consider taking classes or programs to help you. Move forward in developing an effective leadership model by becoming a person of influence.
   - Develop strategies to get out of debt and learn to make prudent investment choices. Be mindful of what it means to be a steward of the blessings God has provided. God can provide mentors who have experience and can help you in this area.
   - Become a better friend to those you have wronged. Ask forgiveness and move on. If you have outgrown old friends, make new friends. Forgive those old friends for their misperceptions and move on. It's hard, I know. But let it go.

33

- Be open to God's direction for your future. God is interested in helping you achieve your heart's desire. Through prayer and action God will assist you in discovering where you would be most fulfilled, most content, and most proficient. Outline a plan of action and move on.
- Identify the areas where you can become the greatest influence in family and church matters. Take action under God's guidance through prayerful direction. Don't think inside the box. If you are a box thinker—get out of the box! Take the risk and develop your ministry under God's leadership. If box thinkers want to remain stuck, then move on.

A Measure of Heaven on Earth by Trusting God

"Trust in the Lord with all of thine heart, and lean not unto thine own understanding. In all thy ways acknowledge him, and he shall direct thy paths."

(Proverbs 3:5)

Let's create another comparison chart.

Heaven	Earth
• Freedom in spirit and soul (outside the box)	• Confinement (in the box)
• Total fulfillment (ascending)	• Walls of defense (descending)
• Unlimited possibilities (complete faith)	• Localities (remaining a victim)

The preceding chart outlines the primary difference between faith and fate. To have a measure of heaven on earth, trust and faith in Jesus, the Son of God, is the essential ingredient. Peaceful living is defeated when we remain confined to the world's way of doing things, remain on the defense, and remain a victim or slave to whatever gives us a false sense of security. Being overly influenced by the world, being human, and living without God are things that keep us victims in life. To remain a victim is to remain useless, helpless, disillusioned, and hopeless. Remember the biblical concept of sowing and reaping. Sowing trouble reaps disaster. Jesus sets us free from this darkness. But we must learn to trust Him. Trusting in God and His son sets life in the right direction? What we trust in will either pave the way to greater blessing or potential disaster. The best way to achieve a goal and gain consistent direction in life is to develop trust. The most effective way to move through the obstacles of life is by trust. Trust always operates in the present tense and helps us move forward to conquer the mountains of life. Faith is required for trust to develop—faith in God's ability to work all things out for good and to benefit our lives. It is a difficult concept and requires time and patience to develop.

A Young Man's Misplaced Treasure

In Luke 18:18–30 Jesus talked about this same challenge with a young man who was very wealthy and didn't see the need for help. The young man comes to Jesus and asks, "What must I do to have this eternal treasure You speak of?" He wanted this treasure. He had every other kind of treasure, and it seemed this treasure was not attainable by the same means he was accustomed to. Jesus told him that he was to follow the commandments. The young man assured Him that he had done that from his youth. Then Jesus told the young man that he lacked one thing. He told him to sell all that he had and give it to the poor. Then he would have treasures in heaven and could come and follow Jesus.

The young man felt defeated because he had great trust in his wealth and wasn't ready to sacrifice it all for Jesus. Jesus was basically telling him that he was to cease putting his reliance upon earthly things that end up as dust. Jesus was telling him of a sure trust that doesn't fade when this earthly existence comes to a close. In the same passage Jesus encouraged those who heard His instructions to the young man and admonished them by telling them that things that are seen as impossible by men are possible with God. He further stated that there is not one individual who, if he left all behind for the sake of God's kingdom, would be left lacking. Jesus was saying that if your trust is in the things of God, many more blessings than you have at this present time will be received. What's more, you shall receive the blessings of all eternity. What an incredible promise! Can you see the larger purpose of God? When we trust, we see God doing things here and now. God's way is invisible unless we are ready to receive such great blessings. When we trust, we realize that God is able to do anything and regards them as being already done. When we develop trust in God, we are able to begin to discern those on earth who are worthy of our trust.

Trust allows us to experience freedom in our souls and spirits that removes insecurities and confinement. We will no longer settle for living inside the box. We no longer view obstacles as defeat, but rather we keep our eyes on the goal. Henry Ford once said, *"Obstacles are the frightful things that happen when we take our eyes off of the goal."* The goal of the Christian is to keep his or her eyes on Jesus and trust Him for everything. What can we expect from developing such a dynamic trust? The possibilities are unlimited. Faith moves mountains when there is complete and unwavering trust.

Talk to the One who cares about your cares. *"Be anxious for nothing, but in everything by prayer and supplication, with thanksgiving, let your requests be made known unto to God; and the peace of God which surpasses all understanding, will guard your hearts and minds through Christ Jesus"* (Phil. 4:6–7). Bring it all to the One who can give you the solution, the keys, the resolution, and peace. The following is a prayer asking for God's complete peace in spite of the anxieties that you face just now.

A Helpful Prayer

> *Oh God, I lift to You the greatest concerns of life. Take my anxieties and fears and convert them into trust and peace. Help me to be mindful of the things I need to change in order to be a better servant of You. Help me to get out of the box and be open by faith to whatever improvements You desire for me. Help me to ascend to Your throne through faith, prayer, and complete trust through every obstacle and challenge of my life. As the Serenity prayer says, "God grant me the serenity to accept things I cannot change, the courage to change the things I can, and the wisdom to know the difference." Grant me trust and peace that I may glorify You in all things. In trusted and blessed name of Jesus, I pray. Amen!*

The Road to Healing

When we experience pain, most of us want immediate relief. However, there are deeper pains that lodge within us and fester over time, causing more devastating illness, the loss of hope, and spiritual death. Total healing is not just relief from physical suffering. Even when we continue to suffer from physical ailments, we can still experience healing on a spiritual level. Medical science tells us there are many incurable diseases that can kill the body. However, medical science does not deal effectively with the diseases of the spirit and soul—the very essence of life. Where do we turn when we are given crushing news regarding our physical health? The human tendency is to react rather than respond. A diagnosis of cancer can cause a fear reaction instead of a faith response. God understands this, and He is there to bring comfort and care. The greatest healing from a devastating disease such as cancer is accomplished in the soul and spirit of the individual. I have seen amazing outcomes because the soul and spirit aspect of healing is the focus. Bitter individuals succumb to the disease quickly with little hope of restoration to family members. This is an unfortunate result that happens too frequently. Cancer can steal the essence of life and breed hopelessness that takes away the life of the soul and spirit. I have many patients who are fighting cancer, but I have very few patients who give up. The key is to fight. Life is worth the battle against a potentially fatal illness. But how do we fight? To whom do we turn when our defenses are weak? We must turn to the supernatural existence of God. We must reach out to God and ask for His divine intervention through prayer and diligent search. We must seek His answers through His Word and the guidance He gives through others whom we trust—family, friends, our physician, or a clergyman. God gives life and He gives it abundantly. When we take the steps to allow God to bring healing to our innermost being, we have the assurance that the outcome will be an excellent one.

Which Path to Follow?

Believe that life is worth living and your belief will help create the fact.

(William James)

To be healed from sickness and disease, we must focus on the precious gift of life. We must turn away from our old patterns of living and be transformed into a new existence. This transformation will include life-giving fruit, such as love, peace, joy, kindness, and faith. Jesus taught: *"For verily I say unto you, That whosoever shall say unto this mountain, Be thou removed, and be thou cast into the sea; and shall not doubt in his heart, but shall believe that those things which he saith shall come to pass; he shall have whatsoever he saith"* (Mark 11:23).

Faith is the belief that we will possess what we hope for. Faith healing is not superstition, nor is it accomplished through the efforts of one person. Healing comes from God and God alone. There is a woman mentioned in the Bible who had a bleeding disorder for many years. She had gone to many physicians and was helped by none of them. She said, "If I may touch but his clothes, I shall be whole" (Mark 5:25–28). What a powerful example of faith. The key is to believe in the *source* of all perfect healing—God himself!

There are many healers in this day and age. Many of them draw from powers that are dark and oppressive. I call them pseudo-healers (false healers), and often the healing is associated with ritual rather than God. I have seen many Christians deceived by healers who call themselves God's messengers. They employ gimmicks and sly tactics to catch individuals off guard by assuring them that what they are about to receive is from God himself and that it is His will for wholeness and the elimination of suffering. The healing that comes from God is free from sly and subtle deceptions, it lasts for all eternity, there are no negative effects, and individuals are not required to make monthly payments. The supposed healing experience at the hands of false healers gives a distorted and confused message on the healing work of the Holy Spirit. The Bible tells us that we are to test the spirits and discern falsehoods by the fruits they produce. Large crowds and great followings are not evidence of spiritual fruit.

The Best Source of Medicine

In Proverbs 4:20–22, the Scripture tells us that the words spoken from the mouth of God are life giving. Reading and growing in God's Word is the best medicine. This doesn't mean that we discard medical science. The Word of God will help us discern the best course for our healing, what action will be appropriate and have the best outcome, and how to proceed. When we are diligent students of His Word, we gain wisdom and understanding. The Holy Spirit guides us and keeps us safe from potential harm. Not only is our faith in His healing ability made stronger, but also our understanding deepens and we develop prudence in our decision-making. The Word of God is the first source of medicine.

Anger, Forgiveness, and Yesterdays

Many times anger is generated because of past failures or hurts. I am reminded of the life of a former president. He had many setbacks in his political life, and he would not let the yesterdays rest. During public appearances he espoused that it was essential not to be defeated by issues from the past. However, when he was alone he became very melancholy over what the press had done to him, what his political rivals did to him, and what the people of America did to him. He couldn't let it go, and he became embittered, enraged, and depressed. It eventually shattered his life, health, and happiness. The power of forgiveness is strong and provides a way of escape. The power of forgiveness offers healing and the ability to forgive. To be forgiven and to forgive are life-giving gifts from the Master Forgiver! Oswald Chambers, an influential and devoted follower of God, illustrates for us the power of God's forgiveness through the work of His Son Jesus Christ. God's interest is to restore life and renew it. When battling illness, life must be restored, peace offered, and anger over the past resolved. Here are Chambers' inspiring words:

> Through the Redemption God undertakes to deal with a man's past, and He does it in two ways: by forgiving him, and by making the past a wonderful culture for the future. The forgiveness of God is a bigger miracle than we are apt to think. It is impossible for a human being to forgive; and it is because this is not realized that we fail to understand that the forgiveness of God is a miracle of Divine grace. Do I really believe that God cannot, dare not, must not forgive me my sin without its being atoned for? If God were to forgive me my sin without its being atoned for, I should have a greater sense of justice than God. It is not that God says in effect, "I will pay no more attention to what you have done." When God forgives a man, He not only alters him but transmutes what he has already done. Forgiveness does not mean merely that I am saved from sin and made right for heaven; forgiveness means that I am forgiven into a recreated relationship to God. Do I believe that God can deal with my "yesterday," and make it as though it had never been? I either do not believe He can, or I do not want Him to. Forgiveness, which is so easy for us to accept, cost God the agony of Calvary. When Jesus Christ says "Sin no more," He conveys the power that enables a man not to sin any more, and that power comes by right of what He did on the Cross. That is the unspeakable wonder of the forgiveness of God. Today men do not bank on what Jesus Christ can do, or on the miraculous power of God; they only look at things from their side—"I should like to be a man or a woman after God's heart, but look at the mountain of my past that is in the way." God has promised to do the thing which, looked at from the basis of our own reason, cannot be done. If a man will commit his "yesterday" to God, make it irrevocable, and bank in confidence on what Jesus Christ has done, he will know what is meant by spiritual mirth—"Then was our mouth filled with laughter, and our tongue with singing." Very few of us get there because we do not believe Jesus Christ means what He says. "It is impossible! Can Jesus Christ re-make me, with my meanness and my criminality; re-make not only my actual life, but my mind and my dreams?" Jesus said, "With God all things are possible." The reason God cannot do it for us is because

of our unbelief; it is not that God won't do it if we do not believe, but that our commitment to Him is part of the essential relationship.[3]

Don't hang on to the pain of the past any longer. Give up those yesterdays and let it go. Let God move you and heal you of the deepest wounds. Let Him make you whole.

Prayer: The Best Strategy

Our healing is not only a journey. It is a battle. In the book of Job, we have a clear illustration of the battle that is waged for our very existence. This battle for life must be fought with powerful methods. Prayer is the most powerful method we have. God is our only true source of life, and He alone has the power over it. God is aware of the battle; and through prayer His power is released to defeat the unseen forces of evil. He does battle for us. He did battle for Job. Through the process life lessons are learned. Read the book of Job. It is an intriguing account of God's power, deliverance, and healing. Prayer is the first place of communication with God. E. M. Bounds, a prayer warrior of the Nineteenth and early Twentieth Century states:

> *"Everything was possible to the men and women who knew how to pray, and it is still possible today. Prayer, indeed opened a limitless storehouse, and God's hand withheld nothing. Prayer introduced those who practiced it into a world of privilege, and brought the strength and wealth of heaven down to the aid of finite man. What rich and wonderful prayer they heard who had learned the secret of victorious approach to God."*[4]

As we pray, it is essential to remember that through the power of God the battle is won. In and of ourselves, we are powerless. We must do all we can, but the power to overcome belongs to God; and when we rely upon Him, we find deliverance from the oppressive forces of sickness and disease. Our prayers do not have to be complicated dissertations, but rather, simple words of faith. Oswald Chambers gives us further insight:

> So far we have been dealing with the aspects of prayer which are more or less easy of statement; we enter now into an aspect which is more difficult to state. Prayer is the outcome of our apprehension of the nature of God, and the means whereby we assimilate more and more of His mind. We must here remind ourselves again of the fundamental matters of our Christian relationship, viz. that in a Christian, faith and common sense are molded in one person by devotion to the mastership of Jesus Christ. This necessitates not conscious adherence to principles, but concentrated obedience to the Master. Faith does not become its own object, that produces fanaticism; but it becomes the means whereby God unveils His purposes to us (see Romans 12:2). Our Lord in instructing the disciples in regard to prayer presented them with three pictures (see Luke 11:1–13; 18:1–8†), and strangely puzzling pictures they are until we understand their meaning. They are the pictures of an unkind friend, an unnatural father, and an unjust judge. Like many of our Lord's answers, these pictures seem no answer at all at first, they seem evasions, but we find that in answering our inarticulate questions our Lord presents His answer to the reality discernible to conscience, and not to logic.[5]

A Prayer of Healing

> Oh God, provide complete healing and deliverance from this affliction and restore me physically, emotionally, and spiritually. Facilitate healing energy within my body and renew every cell and body system through the name and power of Jesus Christ and the power of His blood. Holy Spirit, I cry out to You in this time of affliction. I know that I am within Your care and that this affliction will eventually reveal a greater purpose of God in my life journey. Manifest Your comforting presence and give me faith, grace, and strength to stand in suffering, and may all who see me see You. Protect me from false perceptions and judgments of others. Remove from me the constant desire to vindicate myself and may Your divine truth

be manifested. For this present suffering doesn't compare with what the Lord Jesus Christ has accomplished for me on the cross! Into Your hands I commit this fragile life and wait for Your healing. Replace this broken down body with Your wholeness and renewed strength. You love and accept me as I am. All of my imperfections and weaknesses are before You. Yet You unconditionally love me and adopt me as Your own. You say in Your Word that Your strength is made perfect in weakness. Thank You, God, for loving me as I am and giving me more of Your grace to overcome! I claim Your Word and pray these things in the power of the Holy Spirit. Amen.

The Healing Love of God

Our wonderful, loving God accepts us where we are, and the best of His nature is given to us. When you are lonely and forsaken, the perfect gentleman fatherhood of God and the loving mother's heart of God comforts, cares, rescues, and stabilizes. God meets us where we are. Jesus stands at the door and knocks, the Bible tells us. There is no intrusion or invasion of privacy. The boundaries are not violated. He gently and lovingly comes and asks to be invited in to fill that lonely, desert place. He transforms and restores with the streams of gentle love and holds our hands, walks along with us, and even carries us when we are weak. What other friend will do this for you? When others fail you, He sustains. When others disappoint, He encourages. When others hurt, He heals. When the burden becomes too great, He carries. Embrace the love of God and take it into the loneliest place of your heart. You will find the Friend of all friends and the greatest love of all. Jesus the risen Lord gives the greatest love that heals a multitude of hurts!

The Healing Rest of God

"Come unto me, all ye that are weary and heavy laden, and I will give you rest."

(Matthew 11:28)

God has outlined for us an absolute concept of rest. It is for the weary, burdened, and distressed. I say that this is an absolute concept because the principles of it do not change. This rest cannot be purchased with money. It is not a vacation to the Bahamas. It is not sleeping fourteen hours a day. Another human does not extend it. God extends this rest to us through His divine resources. A perfect illustration of this is found in the prophet Elijah's life experience. Elijah was tired and worn out from the heavy burdens that he carried for many years. He was human, and there was no possible way he could continue to shoulder the heavy burdens. God knew that Elijah needed this perfect rest. The following passage in 1 Kings 17:1–16 outlines this for us:

And Elijah the Tishbite, who was of the inhabitants of Gilead, said unto Ahab, As the LORD God of Israel liveth, before whom I stand, there shall not be dew nor rain these years, but according to my word. And the word of the LORD came unto him, saying, Get thee hence, and turn thee eastward, and hide thyself by the brook Cherith, that is before Jordan. And it shall be, that thou shalt drink of the brook; and I have commanded the ravens to feed thee there. So he went and did according unto the word of the LORD: for he went and dwelt by the brook Cherith, that is before Jordan. And the ravens brought him bread and flesh in the morning, and bread and flesh in the evening; and he drank of the brook. And it came to pass after a while, that the brook dried up, because there had been no rain in the land. And the word of the LORD came unto him, saying, Arise, get thee to Zarephathc, which belongeth to Zidon, and dwell there: behold, I have commanded a widow woman there to sustain thee. So he arose and went to Zarephath. And when he came to the gate of the city, behold, the widow woman was there gathering of sticks:

45

and he called to her, and said, Fetch me, I pray thee, a little water in a vessel, that I may drink. And as she was going to fetch it, he called to her, and said, Bring me, I pray thee, a morsel of bread in thine hand. And she said, As the LORD thy God liveth, I have not a cake, but an handful of meal in a barrel, and a little oil in a cruse: and, behold, I am gathering two sticks, that I may go in and dress it for me and my son, that we may eat it, and die. And Elijah said unto her, Fear not; go and do as thou hast said: but make me thereof a little cake first, and bring it unto me, and after make for thee and for thy son. For thus saith the LORD God of Israel, The barrel of meal shall not waste, neither shall the cruse of oil fail, until the day that the LORD sendeth rain upon the earth. And she went and did according to the saying of Elijah: and she, and he, and her house, did eat many days. And the barrel of meal wasted not, neither did the cruse of oil fail, according to the word of the LORD, which he spake by Elijah.

God fed, comforted, and restored Elijah in an unusual way. As Elijah began to experience greater restoration, he was brought to this widow and depended upon her for further care. In return, this woman and her son were blessed with abundance during a time of great famine in the land. Remember, God foretold this through the prophet Elijah. In unexpected ways and means, God restored Elijah. The widow and her son demonstrated a greater faith and trust in divine sustenance. It is a dimension that can be learned only by complete surrender and submission, even when God's way is not fully understood. We all need this at some time during our earthly journey. When illness comes, a greater dependence upon God is necessary in order to experience complete wholeness. This rest we receive is given as a blessing from God. *"Come unto me, all ye that are weary and heavy laden, and I will give you rest."* Matthew Henry, a respected commentator on God's Word, defines this concept of rest:

"If Providence calls us to solitude and retirement, it becomes us to acquiesce; when we cannot be useful we must be patient, and when

we cannot work for God we must sit still quietly for him. How he was fed. Though he could not work there, having nothing to do but to meditate and pray (which would help to prepare him for his usefulness afterwards), yet he shall eat, for he is in the way of his duty, and verily he shall be fed, in the day of famine he shall be satisfied."

It is essential for you to know God on a personal level before you will understand His power, His grace, His rest, and His sustenance. Jesus said, *"If ye abide in me, and my words abide in you, ye shall ask what ye will, and it shall be done unto you"* (John 15:7). Jesus died so we may live. In order to know Him we must denounce our old patterns of living, forsake our yesterdays, accept His saving grace, and become a follower of His way. His power is available for your healing. May God bless and heal you completely in body, soul, and spirit, and may your life be filled with peace, joy, and hope until His coming. Amen!

CHAPTER THREE

The Foundation of All Healing

"I must tell you in all humility that Hinduism, as I know it, entirely satisfies my soul, fills my whole being, and I find a solace in the Bhagavad and Upainshads that I miss even in the Sermon on the Mount. My days are numbered. I am not likely to live very long— perhaps a year or a little more. For the first time in fifty years I find myself in the slough of despond. All about me is darkness; I am praying for light."

Gandhi

This quote by Gandhi reveals the truth that only the light of God through Jesus can satisfy the longing of the spirit. Gandhi was a religious man, and he believed Jesus to be one of the greatest teachers. Gandhi was a great liberator of the people of India and stood against the social injustices. His mission was to promote peace and humanitarian aid to the needy people of his nation. Jesus spoke of this message of peace and benevolence toward each other and devotion to God in the Sermon on the Mount. Moreover, Jesus modeled what He preached and set in motion the ability of others to live out the Ten Commandments. The light of God expels the darkness of which Gandhi speaks, and the Sermon on the Mount reveals this light. The key is to embrace the Holy Spirit's power to live in the light of God and find peace in the choice of accepting the work of the Savior.

The Fabric of a Satisfied Life

The Sermon on the Mount reveals the code of being fully satisfied. The Greek word for *blessed* translates to mean *fully satisfied.* As I pondered this, I read the Sermon on the Mount with more prayer and discovered that Jesus gives the secret of living a satisfied life in this portion of Scripture. There is a close relationship between being fully satisfied and experiencing health. In life we will encounter both positive and negative experiences. The positive experiences are happily welcomed. The negative life experiences may distract, defeat, and jeopardize our state of total wellness. It is during these negative life experiences that we learn the most about God. Job learned that it was essential to fall back on the strong, loving arm of God as he faced affliction, whether he understood it or not. Life may not make sense to us sometimes, but God always works His miraculous light through it all. I will outline for you the nature of our Lord's teaching on living the fully satisfied life.

The Essential Steps of a Fully Satisfied Life

The Sermon on the Mount begins with Jesus proclaiming blessings. As mentioned previously, the word *blessed* translates from the Greek *fully satisfied.* This doesn't mean to be happy, because happiness depends upon circumstance and situation. What Jesus proclaimed was a message of joy—joy of the Lord that is strong and unmovable. Joy is not temperamental or shaky. It lasts for eternity. This message was for Jesus' followers during New Testament times. And it is for us today. What God has so successfully communicated through His Son is that this message is for the generations to come until the end of the world. John Wesley eloquently articulates this:

> Nor was it only those multitudes who were with him on the mount, to whom he now taught the way of salvation; but all the children of men; the whole race of mankind; the children that were yet unborn; all the generations to come, even to the end of the world, who should ever hear the words of this life.[6]

The Teaching that Prepares the Way for Healing

The Sermon on the Mount is not only a literary masterpiece; it is a summation of God's Divine Code of the human self and human relations. It is the true fabric that knits together the human experience of health, benevolence, and humanitarianism with God's purposeful design for His most intelligent order of creation, man. The following passage in Matthew 5:3–1–48 reveals the beginning point of the above:

- **Poor in Spirit:** To be fully satisfied is to realize one's own spiritual helplessness. *"Blessed are the poor in spirit: for theirs is the kingdom of heaven."*
- **Mournful:** To be fully satisfied is to have sorrow for wrong actions and choices of self and others. Anything that offends God, breaks His moral code, and brings harm to others is considered a wrong action and choice. *"Blessed are they that mourn: for they shall be comforted."*
- **Meekness:** To be fully satisfied is to see yourself as you really are and to have personal submission to God, His Word, and its relation to expressing love and compassion to our neighbor. *"Blessed are the meek: for they shall inherit the earth."*

- **Spiritual Hunger:** To be fully satisfied is to have a continuous satisfaction with God's righteousness with a consistent refilling and replenishment of spiritual strength. *"Blessed are they which do hunger and thirst after righteousness: for they shall be filled."*
- **Merciful:** To be fully satisfied is to have compassion and sympathy. The sorrows of others are heartfelt and motivate to more earnest prayer and support under God's purposeful leadership. *"Blessed are the merciful: for they shall obtain mercy."*
- **Heart Purity:** To be fully satisfied is to experience continuous growth and cleansing of the heart of all that obscures one's view of God. To see God is to be fully satisfied. The sharper one's ability to see God, the more satisfied he or she becomes. *"Blessed are the pure in heart: for they shall see God."*

  Augustine was once accosted by a heathen who showed him his idol and said, "Here is my god; where is thine?" Augustine replied, *"I cannot show you my God; not because there is no God to show but because you have no eyes to see Him."*
- **Peacemaker:** To be fully satisfied is to have the peace of God, which in turn will allow peace to be experienced by fellow human beings. It is not just the ability to stop feuding between nations or people, it is offering solutions and settling disturbing issues in God's timing and within His direction. It is the peace of God that goes beyond human understanding. Yes, this peace can be experienced and modeled in this life. A life disturbed by the action of wars and rumors of wars, the threats of hunger, disaster, failing resources and impending world destruction can embrace the *peace of GOD*. *"Blessed are the peacemakers: for they shall be called the children of God."*

- **Persecuted and Falsely Accused:** To be fully satisfied is to be standing by faith during the toughest times. When persecuted, falsely accused, misperceived, and forsaken by others, God stands with you, never forsaking but continuously defending. This is the highest level of the satisfaction of blessedness. *"Blessed are they which are persecuted for righteousness' sake: for theirs is the kingdom of heaven. Blessed are ye, when men shall revile you, and persecute you, and shall say all manner of evil against you falsely, for my sake. Rejoice, and be exceeding glad: for great is your reward in heaven: for so persecuted they the prophets which were before you."*

The state of being fully satisfied commences when the saving grace of Jesus is taken into the heart and the works of this miracle are manifested in the soul and spirit of the recipient. Anything that pertains to the kingdom of heaven and the rewards of heaven Jesus proclaims in the present tense. This promise is one you can count on.

The Conduit of Healing by Faith

As I read through Matthew 5–7, God spoke to me about the concept of healing. Faith is the strongest conduit the Holy Spirit works through to communicate all healing. It is the foundation required before any works of healing are made manifest. Jesus often referred to faith as being the prime mover of healing. When He said, "Thy faith hath made thee whole," He directed attention away from the miracle itself and placed it upon faith or the lack of faith. This faith foundation places the emphasis on human interaction with God, self, neighbor, and all that exists. A true miracle brought by the Savior requires an understanding of what it means to completely open to God on every level of human existence. The rest of the message of the Sermon will enlighten your heart.

1. **Jesus Proclaims the Way to Healing**

   - **Salt and Light:** Salt has flavor and flavor-enhancing qualities. Light reflected and absorbed is an inescapable form of energy that cannot be hidden. Jesus uses salt and light to get to the senses of our humanity. Our human experience should contain the salt of God's living testimony in our souls and the light of His presence in our spirits.

   - **Living by the Commandments:** A very important reinforcing message that Jesus gave is that the law was not being done away with. A breaking of the commandments and teaching that causes an offense against the law of God have consequences. However, there is an even a stronger requirement of true, living righteousness—not a legalistic, self-serving pious act likened to that of the Scribes and Pharisees. The kingdom of heaven is inaccessible to those who don't have the attribute of God's righteousness imprinted on the fiber of their human existence.

   - **Overcoming Anger:** Part of overcoming anger is promoting peace with all men. The Scripture teaches us that if it is possible we should pursue peace. Forgiveness and anger resolution are the requirements for complete healing. We can break the commandment of "Thou shalt not kill" with our word and thoughts. We may never physically harm another human being, but with our words and the intention of our hearts we may violate this commandment. The key to overcoming anger is God's forgiveness.

   - **Sin in the Heart:** It is not enough to obey the commandment "Thou shall not commit adultery." The thought of adultery is the same as the act of adultery on the sin scale. It is unfortunate that the sensitivity towards this message is often ignored and so called; Many Christians seem to feel it is OK to divorce for any reason. Often, the real reason is because of what the Bible calls the "lust of the eyes, the lust of the flesh, and the pride of life." In 1 Kings chapter 11 the story of David's sin unfolds. In King David's case, sin was in his heart, causing him to commit both adultery and murder. He saw a beautiful woman who was married to a loyal man and lusted for her and committed sexual sin. In order to cover his sin he had the woman's husband killed. Her husband, Uriah, was a noble warrior for the King, and he was a leader that was well respected. As is often the case, the consequences from these acts were terrible for all involved. Sin often has consequences that cause problems for many years after it is originally committed. In an instant, the King, a man after God's own heart, became an adulterer and a murderer. God's faithfulness to forgive is great, but the consequences are irrevocable.

- **Divorce and Marriage:** Divorce rates have been high for several decades. The lack of commitment, loyalty, fidelity, and Christlike love contributes to this disheartening statistic. Often it is lust, greed, and selfishness that are the causes of broken relationships. Our society suffers, our children suffer, our sense of community declines, and God's intended standard for the family is unfulfilled. I hear of many Christian marriages ending in divorce because of what is called incompatibility. I call it foolishness, lack of maturity, and God calls it sin. The Church itself is responsible for this terminology that allows our young people to think that there is a way out of the responsibility of marriage if things don't go their way. God didn't divorce mankind because of consistent disobedience and hurtful acts committed against Him. Another assault on marriage today is society's acceptance of same-gender sexual unions. Worldwide acceptance of this is surely a sign of the degradation of the times. God calls it perversity and unnatural, and it is not at all what He intended for marriage. In God's eyes such a union is against His holy character and pure love. His love is pure and not associated with perverse sexual acts. His compassion never fails, and He desires wholesome natural relationships. His desire is for man and woman to come together in the biblical principle of marriage that is a symbol of His nature and purpose of His Church. Christians should never embrace and tolerate the lifestyle choice of same sex unions. Collectively, the church must stand and oppose every appearance of such perversity and defend God's marriage plan. True healing cannot take place when God's marriage plan is violated and same sex unions are enabled as an acceptable expression of societal change. You can read further on this subject in Dr. James Dobson's book, *Marriage Under Fire*. In this book Dr. Dobson addresses the moral breakdown of God's institute of marriage.

- **Abortion:** The very word can incite many emotions in people. For those who have had an abortion it is an ongoing source of pain and unresolved guilt. Statistics show that most couples, married or unmarried, have a break of relationship after having an abortion. Statistics also show that about 1 in 3 women have had at least one abortion. In other words, it could be your neighbor, your friend, even yourself. There is an answer to the pain and guilt. There is forgiveness and restoration with God through Jesus. There is a healing power that comes through the work of the Holy Spirit.

There are women who, having experienced abortion themselves, want to help others through the healing process. There is an organization, Healing Hearts Ministries, an international ministry devoted to this need with headquarters in Bonney Lake, WA. You may contact them on the Internet for help or information at www.healinghearts.org. Don't bear the pain alone your healing is imminent and the Master is waiting to touch you to make you whole.

- **Acts of Polygamy**: Another violation to God's principle of marriage is polygamy, which is having more than one partner. This is a practice that is coming out of the closet and is practiced with no shame. Polygamy is sin, just as adultery and same sex unions are. Again, open societal acceptance of such violations of God's standards of living demonstrates the degradation of humanity, and the consequences are clearly outlined in God's Holy Scripture. It is necessary to cry out for God's forgiveness and ask that He free individuals who are weighed down by the darkness of these practices to live as He has designed. His desire is for one lifelong marriage between a man and woman, clean and free from sexual perversity.
- **Oaths**: The disappointment of broken promises can scar for a lifetime. Do not promise if you cannot perform. God keeps his promises. When Jesus said, "Let your communication be *yes* or *no*, He meant

that if it is not your intention to fulfill your promises, it is better for you not to promise at all. The God of the unbroken promise takes oath breaking seriously because He keeps His promises.

- **Retaliation:** In his writings, Augustine reflects on the need to be completely liberated from the lust of vindication. Our Lord's solution is for us to not allow anger and bitterness to take hold and for us to forgive—to express love in return for hate. Our natural inclination is to fight to prove that we are right, and in the process we become sick and saddened. The joy of life then becomes depleted, and our view of God can be marred by the fact that justice was not rendered on our terms. The Bible confirms, "The Lord will fight for you and ye shall hold your peace," Exodus14:14. This is hard—but the Lord requires it nonetheless!

- **Enemies:** Loving our friendly neighbor is not a great challenge. Loving our enemy is much harder. Our father requires us to love our enemies, bless those who curse us, do good to them who hate us, and pray for those who despitefully use and persecute us. This is another reinforcement of the state of blessedness.

- **Working for God:** Our labors should be done unto the Lord and not unto men. God is very much in favor of secret works. I often think of the many anonymous Christian sayings and prayers. Did you ever wonder how many of them were written by the hand of God?

Through the centuries, there are many good people who have labored for mankind with no desire for recognition. Some have passed through life without knowing God, but they still rendered works of kindness and compassion. God calls His followers to selflessness.

Gandhi's life experience of achieving good for his people is an example of a labor of love. His desire was for peace and justice. However, the light of God was missing in the labor of this very special man. Gandhi made a sad affirmation of this when he stated that he had read about the Christ of the New Testament and had discovered what a great man this Jesus was. But he was disappointed by the fact that the followers who called themselves Christians were so unlike this Christ. Could it be that this great man failed to see a true witness of Jesus, His power, His love and acceptance, His forgiveness and justice? Or was he so closed to the true light of God's spirit that he failed to see the Master? All fall short of the glory of God, and unless we accept Jesus Christ as Lord and Master, we too will suffer the kind of loneliness Ghandi experienced. There are no exceptions.

- **Prayer and Fasting:** These are two great forces of Christianity that can facilitate the movement of God! He gives us these powerful tools to let us know that through faith, commitment, trust, and action—this being our obligation of service—He will honor and grant our requests. Fasting is also an act of worship and service to God. When fasting for the right purpose, which is drawing closer to God in faith and service, the spirit worship of God becomes strengthened and a stronger bond and union with Him results. Jesus fasted in the wilderness for this purpose.

- **Treasure in Heaven:** All that exists on our planet is temporal. It lasts only for a season. Every day we must praise God for the opportunities He brings and thank Him for His faithfulness in maintaining the promises and blessings of this life. Laboring for things—money, fame, and fortune—is not the same as laboring for the Kingdom of God. The Bible doesn't forbid the *acquiring* of wealth and fortune; it forbids the *worship* of these things. When the focus is on God and His treasures, our commitment is to serve God with the first fruit of all that He has blessed us with. It is all God's property, and seeking Him first affirms our worship and devotion to Him rather than to the world.

- **The Light of the World**: The light of God illuminates the soul and spirit. The darkness of this present world dims the soul and the spirit. If we live our lives by worldly values, we live in descent patterns. Desire for the world and all that is within the world is the same as storing treasures where decay claims the fortune. Treasures in heaven are stored when the attributes of Jesus are put into practice in our lives and the focus is on others and not on self. We must put God's kingdom first and when we do self is not the focus.

- **Put God's Kingdom First**: Jesus said, "No man can serve two masters: for either he will hate the one, and love the other; or else he will hold to the one, and despise the other." Living in an ascent pattern is the same as keeping our focus upon God. If worldly things become more important then a descent pattern is inevitable. As I previously mentioned, a fall is imminent if the things of the world become the focus. Don't be confined to the box of "it's about me." Get out of the box and see things from God's larger view of knowing it's all about Him.

2. Jesus is Building on a Firm Foundation

The healing ministry of Jesus is built on the firm foundation established by God the Father. In Matthew chapter eight He reveals the power of this ministry. All of the miracles performed by Jesus demonstrate the power of God. He has the power to forgive sins and cast out demons. The message is clear and leads to salvation and sanctification. Sanctification simply means to be established in the will of God and set apart for His work. These are the building blocks of the Christian life. These are gifts given by God for our healing. Do not be neglectful of this gift of healing, as the nine lepers were. After they received what they wanted, they didn't care to follow the rest of the requirements.

The gift of salvation—a personal relationship with almighty God—is an indescribable gift! Yet how often do we sincerely thank our Lord for all that He has done in making this possible? Our lack of praise and thanksgiving for His gift of salvation can be likened to the response of the ten lepers after being miraculously healed by Christ (Luke 17:11–19). Only one returned to express gratitude. The other nine were more interested in what had happened to them personally than in remembering the One who had performed the miracle. Are you ever guilty of lack of gratitude? It is interesting to imagine the life-long remorse brought about by such ingratitude:

> *I meant to go back, but you may guess I was filled with amazement, I cannot express; To think that after those horrible years, that passion of loathing and passion of fears;*

Of sores unendurable—eaten, defiled—my flesh was as smooth as the flesh of a child; I was drunk with joy; I was crazy with glee; I scarcely could walk and I scarcely could see; For the dazzle of sunshine where all had been black; but I meant to go back; Oh, I meant to go back! I had thought to return, when people came out; there were tears of rejoicing and laughter and shout; My cup was so full I seemed nothing to lack! But I meant to go back, Oh, I meant to go back![7]

The Light of God Satisfies

The light of the world is Jesus. This light is clearly illustrated in the account of Nicodemus. This man came to Jesus by night, probably for fear of being caught by his fellow Pharisee colleagues, affirming that Jesus was in fact more than just a great teacher by the evidence of the signs and wonders that He performed. Oswald Chambers gives some insight on the discourse that Jesus had with Nicodemus on what it means to be born again: "Jesus answered and said to him, Most assuredly, I say to you, unless one is born again, he cannot see the kingdom of God"—John 3:3 (NKJV).

"A man cannot take in anything he has not begun to think about, consequently until a man is born again what Jesus says does not mean anything to him. The Bible is a universe of revelation facts, which have no meaning for us until we are born from above; when we are born again we see in it what we never saw before. We are lifted into the realm where Jesus lives and we begin to see what He sees."[8]

It is the light of God that satisfies that comes from Jesus our Lord. He illuminates our path and gives the hope of eternal blessedness. When we see what He sees, life will have more meaning and purpose.

Resisting the Darkness of this World

The light of God through His Son Jesus Christ and the work of the Holy Spirit breaks the curse of this present darkness. Many times Jesus said not to love the things of this world. He also taught that light has nothing in common with darkness. In our human experience we may struggle with dark patterns of behavior, thoughts, and habit. It is God's desire to change old patterns, and they certainly cannot be changed by our limited human strength. It requires supernatural deliverance from the old ways of doing things and practicing the peace and holiness of God. Darkness can go back for generations, and there may be some things that you do that you just can't figure out. The Apostle Paul speaks of this pattern in Romans 7. In this passage Paul affirms that it is the power of darkness at work that disables him from carrying out what he knows in his heart to be right and true. He also affirms that it is the carnal state of humans to give in to such behavior. It is God's desire to bring it to light to help us overcome and be set free. The Bible tells us that Jesus came to set the captives free. It makes no difference how long an individual is a Christian if there is a residue of dark patterns remaining. Throughout our lives, the perfection of God is necessary to overcome our innate weaknesses. He heals us by setting us free from the things that hold us captive. He breaks the curse of darkness by the light of His presence. Then we are lifted to the place where Jesus lives, and we see what He sees.

CHAPTER FOUR

The Deep Wounds of Betrayal and Denial

"But Jesus said to him, "Judas are you betraying the Son of Man with a kiss?."

(Luke 22:48 NKJV)

"'I have sinned by betraying innocent blood,' . . . Then he threw down the pieces of silver in the temple and departed, and went and hanged himself."

(Matthew 27:4–5 NKJV)

"And the Lord turned and looked at Peter. Then Peter remembered the word of the Lord, how He had said to Him, 'Before the rooster crows, you will deny Me three times.' So Peter went out and wept bitterly."

(Luke 22:61–62 NKJV)

Deep Wounds

Betrayal and denial inflict deep wounds. Peter said that he would never forsake his Lord. He was about to be tested greatly; Jesus foretold that it all would happen soon.

Of course, Peter had no idea what was ahead, and he certainly wasn't aware of the deep deficiency housed in his soul. Certainly, he was going to have a chance to prove his fidelity and love for the Master in ways he had never counted on. Jesus prepared him and said the enemy of his soul's desire was to sift him. Jesus lifted this man in prayer to the throne of His Father and gave Peter the assurance that he would come out on top and overcome this deep-seated spiritual weakness. God provides a way of escape; all that is required is that we take it by seeking His forgiveness and surrender our human weaknesses completely to Him.

Judas, on the other hand, demonstrated the resistant human spirit to the core. Jesus first elaborated on the events that were going to take place at the Last Supper. Jesus sat with both his betrayer and denier and did not condemn. Although He knew their intentions, He provided the way of escape even then. Yes, He knew what was going to happen, but forgiveness was already set in motion. Guilt and pride gave birth to the greatest sins of all—betrayal and denial. The dark forces of evil were at work in Judas. His desire for approval and recognition was greater than his desire for humble, quiet service to his Master. Peter's cowardly behavior darkened his reasoning to the point that he was not truthful.

The Judas and Peter in Us All

I remember many things about growing up in the Bronx. One thing that always stuck with me was that I didn't want to end up like Judas. I grew up Roman Catholic, and it wasn't until I accepted Jesus by personal faith that God gave me clarity. The Roman Catholic way of looking at it was wrong, and I had much anger about the crucifixion and the betrayal of Jesus. I was angry at the injustice of what happened to Jesus as I was angry about the injustices of the environment of the Bronx. Even though the Bronx was a rough place to grow up, there was a loyalty code, and to be a Judas was really bad. I heard the phrase, "Don't be a Judas" on many occasions. I got the strong message from family, the Catholic church, and acquaintances that being a Judas was the ultimate sin against God. When I accepted Jesus into my heart, I realized that the same dark forces that were at work in Judas and Peter were at work in me also, and the acceptance of the resurrection work of my Lord was necessary for me to be free from the underlying sin that would keep me bound to this carnal nature.

There is a Judas and Peter in us all: greed, envy, pride, anger, rebellion, denial, and betrayal. How many times have you introspectively said, like some of the disciples, *Is it I?* This is called human weakness, and God makes himself perfect in our weakness when we surrender to Him. Judas and Peter had opportunity to turn over their guilt and great anguish of heart to God in complete surrender. God did not doom Judas or Peter. Judas doomed himself and left himself no escape from his terrible act of betrayal. Peter floundered for many days in darkness and depression as a result of his lying and denying. Jesus prayed for all of the disciples because He knew the tests they were going to face. He knew the challenge that Judas faced and loved him just as much as He loved Peter, John, and the others. The opportunity for transformation presented itself to Judas. This transformation would have turned those dirty thirty pieces of silver into the finest gold in an instant! The love of God covers a multitude of sins as it did when King David committed adultery and murder and when the Apostle Paul killed followers of Jesus. It took a complete breakdown and surrender of self and the experience of getting down to the rock bottom of self and the acceptance that the only way out is by the work of the risen Christ!

The Pattern of Betrayal and Denial

When betrayal and denial are displayed in our attitudes, habits, and daily actions, we hurt people. Were you ever hurt by someone's careless attitude or neglect of the important things of life? Doing to others what you would desire them to do to you is not just a wise old saying, it is found in the Scripture as a rule for living.

A common attitude is "Get what you can, step on people in the process, wait until age has taken its course, and then possibly seek forgiveness from the ones who were hurt by your behavior." Jesus always forgives us when we ask; however, waiting until the last season of life to change our hurtful behaviors results in regrets and guilt that will plague our remaining time on the planet. Judas, instead of going back and crying out for mercy and forgiveness, chose not to face the truth of his betraying God through deception, cunning, and greed, and that was his mark on history. He hung himself, believing the lie that God would not forgive him because his act was beyond the point of hope. In Judas's frame of mind, the only way out was to take his own life. If he had waited, he would have seen that the Savior was about to give His life in exchange for the act of betrayal and extend forgiveness and love. Judas's life was given to him as a gift from God; however, Judas was his own god and he called the shots—a big mistake. The blood of Jesus was spilled to pay the penalty for such sin. Don't allow the patterns of betrayal and denial to take hold and keep you bound. Remember the cowardly act of Judas as an example. Also remember that God provided the way of escape and that Judas failed to take it. Peter embraced it and was forgiven. It is your choice whether or not to break the old familial patterns of sinful behavior.

Denial breeds a dependence upon dysfunctional behavior patterns that keep old family habits alive. Break them. You can hold to the power of God and break the pattern of dysfunctional behavior in your family line. These dysfunctional behaviors come in many varieties: self-centeredness, greed, pride, sexual lust and perversity, meanness, an unforgiving spirit, and many others. Denial is the same as lying to oneself about the deeper issues that need corrective measures and change.

In contrast, Peter accepted responsibility for his actions, broke down, and surrendered to God. As soon as the cock crowed he remembered the words of Jesus; the gaze of God pierced his soul and spirit, leaving no room for ignorance, neglect, or excuses. He wept bitterly because he knew he failed God. His deep desire was to please Him. He had hurt his Master, and there was no way to tell Him to His face that he was sorry because the events happened quickly. However, God is so good that He met with Peter and John afterwards and gave them the promise of the Holy Spirit as the comfort and guide and that they would be shown all truth. The deeper learning and change was about to come upon all who had opportunity to serve Jesus while He lived. For sure, Peter, John, and the rest of the apostles were going to be given the opportunity to prove their faith, obedience, and maturity. Peter died for his God. He went the distance, and Jesus met him there. I can hear Jesus saying to Peter as he entered the gates of glory, "Peter, I prayed for you and had faith in you always. I knew you were going to make the ultimate sacrifice for me. You gave your life to serve me as I gave my life to set you free from the stronghold and pull of the world. I love you Peter, always have, forever for eternity, I am glad you're here." Judas would have heard the same words from Jesus as we all have; "Father, forgive them for they know not what they do."

When Betrayal and Denial Hurts Me

When we are on the receiving end of betrayal and denial, we can experience deep wounds that can take many years to overcome. Have you ever been betrayed by a friend? Maybe you thought that your friendship was inseparable and solid. Then some misunderstanding or communication shift spoiled the friendship. It hurts, and it seemed that the more you tried to communicate, the worse the situation became. Maybe you tried calling, e-mailing, writing letters, and trying to meet face-to-face, but it was to no avail. Or maybe a parent, son, daughter, brother, or sister betrayed you despite your selfless love and forgiving spirit. The terrible hurt can last for years. Jesus experienced this kind of deep hurt from the two men in whom He invested a selfless love. What do you do when you have invested a selfless love and it is exploited by betrayal and denial? Jesus said from the cross, "Father, forgive them." This is the only way to begin to heal from the hurt that was etched upon your soul. In this forgiveness you experience a freedom to pursue a new dimension of relationship with God and others. In addition, you are leaving the door open for another opportunity to restore a friend or one you deeply love. God is not only a God of second chances, He is the God of unlimited opportunity. There is no chance associated with His nature. It is all divine design and opportunity for restoration, forgiveness, and maturity of the spirit.

The God of Opportunity

While Peter agonized over his failure, he was not able to tell his Master how he really felt. He was filled with guilt and shame, and I'm sure his desire was to tell Jesus all about it. Jesus intended to see Peter again. In John chapter 21 Jesus showed himself to the disciples for the purpose of relinquishing doubt, fear, and guilt. Peter tried to get his mind off things by working harder and returning to what he knew gave him a sense of security. He and the rest of the disciples went fishing. Jesus was standing on the shore waiting for them. He loved those disciples so much, and He knew their hurts. He asked them if they had any food and told them to cast their nets on the right side of the boat and they would find food. There was no question this time; they cast their nets without any hesitation, and there were so many fish that the nets couldn't hold them all. John, the disciple whom Jesus loved, immediately stated to Peter, "It is the Lord!" When Peter heard this from John he plunged into the sea and swam with all of his strength to get to his Master. As he swam, tears of joy and expectancy flooded his soul. He was going to tell Jesus of the love he had for Him. When he met Jesus, not a word was spoken. If there had been, the Bible would have elaborated further. Jesus waited until after breakfast. He ate with the disciples, and none of them asked Him who He was—knowing that it was the Lord. Peter couldn't express what he had rehearsed in his mind as he swam towards Jesus. He remained speechless. Jesus understood him and waited for the right time to have a spirit-to-spirit talk.

A most heart-touching discourse was about to occur. After breakfast, Jesus asked Simon Peter, "Do you love Me?" Peter answered, "Yes," and Jesus said, "Feed My lambs." A second time Jesus asked Peter, "Do you love Me?" Peter said, "You know that I love You." Jesus replied, "Feed My sheep." Then a third time Jesus asked, "Do you love Me?" Peter was grieved because Jesus asked him the third time. Peter received the message clearly and it was no longer his mouth that responded to Jesus—it was his whole being. He told his Master that He knew all things and that he loved Him. Peter had plenty of opportunity to look introspectively after he denied Jesus. When he did respond, he responded with his entire soul and spirit.

Demonstrating Our Love

It was Peter's turn to demonstrate his love to Jesus, and, indeed, throughout the rest of his life, he had the opportunity. Jesus told him that the course of his life and service would take him to the ultimate place of sacrificial love. Tradition has it that Peter was crucified, but not in the same fashion as his Lord. He was crucified upside down because he wanted the world to know that the Savior of the world lives on and that there was only one mediator between God and man, Jesus Christ, the Son of God. Jesus foretold the suffering that would come in John 21: 18–19. *"Verily, verily, I say unto thee, When thou wast young, thou girdedst thyself, and walkedst whither thou wouldest: but when thou shalt be old, thou shalt stretch forth thy hands, and another shall gird thee, and carry thee whither thou wouldest not.' This spake he, signifying by what death he should glorify God. And when he had spoken this, he saith unto him, Follow me."*

An account of great betrayal and hurt is found in Genesis chapter 37 of the Old Testament. Joseph was betrayed and deeply wounded by his brothers.

Likewise, it is our turn to demonstrate our love toward God through the tough times of pain and suffering. Turning betrayal and denial into love and obedience, surrendering all, and allowing the Holy Spirit to heal our wounds is the only way to live peaceably in this life.

Free from the Deep Wounds

Simple steps are outlined below to facilitate a new and healthy relationship with God and others. A story of betrayal in the book of Genesis tells of Joseph's betrayal by his brothers. The ache in his heart was so great that he wept tears of grief and sadness. The betrayal was so hurtful that he could have easily used his power to seek revenge. But he turned his eyes to heaven and offered complete forgiveness. Joseph's brothers suffered from the burden of guilt, fear, and shame for years, and he knew their torment. His statement of what his brothers meant for evil God has meant for good demonstrates Joseph's determination to model the opportunity of loving with a perfect love that casts out all fear, guilt, shame, and insecurity. This same freedom is available for all who embrace the forgiveness and love of God.

- Ask God's forgiveness if you recognize the same patterns of betrayal and denial in your life.
- Forgive those who have betrayed you with the same forgiveness God has extended to you.
- Set your heart on being honest with yourself before God and do not deny your human weakness.
- Do the work required to change the old familial dysfunctional patterns. Like Peter, God will give you the opportunity and the tools required.
- Determine to be in constant communion with God and seek His direction for your life. Accept the healing work of God, which is often based upon the maturity to accept it.

In Joseph and Peter we can observe both the weeping over the deep hurt they experienced and the deep hurt they caused. Peter wept bitterly because he was broken over wounding his Lord. He denied his Lord! This was the ultimate rejection. Joseph wept with brokenness because he was deeply wounded by the betrayal and rejection. In each case the healing power of God's forgiveness is clearly seen. Joseph forgave his brothers just as Jesus forgave mankind, and Peter was forgiven by Jesus who sacrificed His life to demonstrate His love!

CHAPTER FIVE

Practical Steps for Healing

"What will our answer be? Oh let it be a prayer from the depths of our heart, that the living Christ may take each one of us and link us closely to Himself."

(Andrew Murray)

Can God Heal Me? Or Will God Heal Me?

The key to healing is a full belief and trust that God is able and willing to perform the miracle.

Ask yourself, *Do I fully believe that God can heal me? If so, do I trust Him enough to allow Him to perform the miracle?* There are obstacles to healing, and often they are lodged in our souls and spirits. We can become imprisoned and held captive by our human existence and all that encompasses it. Christians are not immune to this. After the fall of mankind, our sheltered and protected existence came to a halt. Jesus came to free us from that mold. He came to offer us empathy and protection from the human viewpoint in a divine and infallible manner.

The beginning point of all healing is to know Him as Savior and Lord. This is the very beginning of the healing of our deepest affliction. Christians have available to them the power of God to break the toughest link in the chain that binds them. When a person accepts and commits his or her entire life to God, much unwanted baggage is unloaded and never again picked up. This is the way it should begin. Along the way some may struggle with the total release of this unwanted cargo, resulting in bondage of soul and spirit. This state is worse than the initial coming to God with a wounded and shattered life and finding relief of the burden and affliction. Typically, it is the process of time that God utilizes to bless the soul and spirit with complete healing.

- **The Word of God**
  The beginning place for genuine healing is the Word of God—the only sure foundation of divine healing. Human reasoning and worldly methods cannot shake this healing. A person's faith in the Word is a summation of belief in the principles of God, the promises of God, and the miraculous working of God.

- **The Will of God**
  It is necessary to be fully assured that it is the will of God to bless you with health of body, mind, and spirit. Trust and confidence that God hears the cry of your heart for healing facilitates the miracle of healing in your life. Nothing is too hard for God. Though one may know this in his or her mind, it is another matter to know this in trust. Trust allows us to know that God has already performed the miracle or blessing and believe that in His time He will allow fulfillment. Vague trust leaves room for doubt, and God's work of healing can be hindered. A doubting mind and spirit counter God's power of healing. Often, disease disappears

when the light of God permeates the area of need in body, mind, and spirit. However, trust and faith are essential in order for such healing power to occur.

> Disease can disappear,
> Minds can be made clear.
> Hearts are lightened,
> Those held captive free.
> True miracles by God's hand,
> They stand the test of time.
> Dependable and sure not as the sand,
> Not by human frailty or intellectual means.
> By the power of God,
> The miracle of divine healing!
>
> —Author Unknown

- **Commit and Claim God's Promise**

  The spirit, soul, and body must be set apart to God and the promise of God claimed. The Scripture teaches us to ask, seek, and knock. All of these imply the necessity of some level of action. Each of these actions requires more work than the previous. In healing, there is work that must be accomplished in the believer before God is free to bestow His promise of healing. There is a big difference between asking and taking, between expecting and accepting. You must take Jesus Christ as your healer—not as an experiment, not as a future benefit, but as a present reality. You must believe that He works now on your behalf. There must be distinct separation between reliance upon human means for healing (self initiated) and the healing of God. Staying in or resorting to old means and patterns of living should never be options. God is the Great Physician, and He will not share His glory with any other. He wants to deliver you from all that wounds and scars the core of your heart and spirit. You can trust Him. He is a gentleman.

- **Pray Faithfully**
  The effectual, fervent prayer of a person serving God and living a life set apart for the purpose of God is powerful. Praying in faith is essential. Through faith we know that God is actively working on our behalf at every moment. Jesus intercedes for us, His children, and actively supports us through the work of the Holy Spirit. As the physician Luke's account of the model prayer that Jesus taught in Luke 11:13 shows us, our heavenly Father will give the Holy Spirit to those who ask Him.

- **Testing of Faith**
  Job realized after significant affliction of body, soul, and spirit that God controls all of nature. His initial cry during the affliction is found in his own words:

  > *"Naked came I from my mother's womb, and naked shall I return, The Lord gave and the Lord hath taken away; blessed be the name of the Lord."*
  >
  > (Job 1:21)

  Job's first response was to fall down and worship God. He did not plead for nature to make intercession. He didn't call on false deities to help him. He didn't use techniques that compromised his faith and integrity. He knew that his only hope was in God. Nature did not and does not do the healing; it is by the power of God. More specifically, the risen Savior Jesus has conquered death. As Job was restored to health and was more blessed by the building of his faith, so the newness of life given through the life sacrifice of Jesus is ours by faith!

> *"For which cause we faint not; but though our outward man perish, yet the inward man is renewed day by day"*
> (2 Corinthians 4:16)

- **Know God Firsthand and Glorify God with Your New Health**

  Don't be like the nine who forgot God. Recognize the miracle of health that God has blessed you with. When Jesus healed, He often told the recipient to proclaim the healing and share the good news with family, friends, and communities. God gives the blessings of life and health and we must proclaim it. Phillip Keller says it eloquently:

  > *"For the person who truly knows God firsthand, there are pleasures forevermore in His presence. There is a sparkle in the eyes. There is a smile on the face. There is a spring in the step, even into old age. There is a cheerful outlook on a world all-awry. There is a bright assurance that our Father is still very much at work behind all the dark clouds of this century. There is a bright hope of heaven and the sure knowledge of sharing in His life forever and forever!"*[9]

CHAPTER SIX

The Holy Temple of Spirit, Soul, and Body

"What? Know ye not that your body is the temple of the Holy Ghost which is in you, which ye have of God, and ye are not your own? For ye are bought with a price: therefore glorify God in your body, and in your spirit, which are God's .

(1 Corinthians 6:19–20)

"Being made in the image of God as persons, Adam and Eve were able to make real choices. They had true creativity, not just in the area we call 'art' but also in the area of choice."

(Francis A. Schaeffer)[10]

We are created in the image of God. We are inscribed on the palm of His hands. You can find this in Isaiah 49:14–16. Recently, the entire genome was mapped. It was originally thought that there were 100,000 genes; it was later discovered that there are 30,000. Not all functions of every gene are known, even though the entire genome is mapped. This creation of God is a complex design of genes and systems that operate in harmony. God's creative work is a harmonious work, and all things work together to promote balance known in science as homeostasis.

Gregor Mendel, an Austrian monk, discovered the foundation of genetics. Mendel deduced the laws of inheritance by studying pea plants in the monastery garden. He observed the characteristics of the development of the plants and noted height, seed shape, and other growth characteristics from one generation of plant to the next. He termed the underlying principles "invisible elements" hidden inside the plants that parent plants passed on to their offspring and that governed the plants' visible features. He came up with rules of how different combinations of elements produce recessive or dominant traits.

Nobody believed Mendel at the time, but his work was rediscovered in 1900 and soon became the foundation for modern genetics. In 1953, two scientists, an American named James Watson and an Englishman named Francis Crick, made a stunning breakthrough and solved the riddles that had perplexed generations of scientists. They revealed the structure of DNA in which two strands twist around each other in the known structure double helix. Each DNA strand is a type of spiral staircase that has specific pairs of molecular components constructed in an orderly and consistent manner. If this order is disrupted in some way it changes the course and sequence and affects virtually every cell in existence. In every human cell, separate spiral DNA staircases comprise each of forty-six chromosomes. Those chromosomes couple up as twenty-three pairs, with one pair mismatched in males. In men, the twenty-third pair consists of X and Y chromosome, making twenty-four unique types of DNA staircases in humans. Our genetic matrix is truly a miracle of God, establishing the fact that human intelligence is not responsible for such discovery. What these two brilliant scientists discovered was already foreknowledge in the mind of God.

We Are a Holy Creation

Dr. Paul Brand's book, *Fearfully and Wonderfully Made*, so beautifully sums the mystery of creation:

> *"It is safe to assume that God enjoys variety, and not just at the cellular level. He didn't stop with a thousand insect species; He conjured up three hundred thousand species of beetles and weevils alone. In His famous speech in the Book of Job, God pointed with pride to such oddities of creation as the mountain goat, the wild ass, the ostrich, and the lightning bolt. He lavished color, design, and texture on the world. People, created in God's image, have continued the process of individualization, grouping themselves according to distinct cultures."*[11]

Our Spiritual Genes

We are the artwork of God. This beautiful work of creation has the inscription, *Made in God's Image*. Make no mistake; this was no accident. As part of the temple of God, we are body, soul, and spirit, and we are created in wholeness. God has fashioned all of the genes that comprise the human species. Thirty thousand genes have been found and some of these genes, in all probability, control emotional and spiritual expressions of our total being. It is a code that God has inscribed into us that cannot be erased. It is His mark of ownership upon us and should be a welcomed one at best. However, the beauty of God's higher creation has been corrupted by sin and shame, thereby, the expressions of a once perfect union broken. Thus, the beginning of physical, emotional, and spiritual sickness and a once perfect genome now has become a broken and deranged genome in need of constant repair and adaptation.

We can have physical, emotional, and spiritual weaknesses that arise from weak links passed down from prior generations. I believe that the genome created by God also encodes behavioral and spiritual traits. Weakness of body, mind, and spirit can be manifested as a result of deranged genes. It is not that God creates bad genes. These genes, once created in perfect harmony, have been altered by the physical, social, and spiritual environments of time. To illustrate this point, an individual struggling with an addiction to alcohol finds it difficult to resist drinking. Often the struggle is rooted in generations of compulsive drinking, which is more than just a physical or emotional sickness. It is an expression of spiritual bondage and adversarial dark forces at work to destroy the precious gift of life for generations. If this soul and spirit weakness propagates and is never remedied by recognition of its root, spiritually it becomes a powerful destructive force. It is my theory that this behavior pattern is an expression of manipulated spiritual genetics by satanic forces to keep an individual from serving God. The knowledge of this behavior is not to be used as an excuse to continue such behavior but for the realization that it takes the power of God along with strict cooperation of the individual to overcome the generational darkness. It is not as simple as quitting the habit any time one wants too. It is not as easy as just going through rehab, a detoxification program, or a "12-Step" program to kick the habit. These may be helpful, but alone they are not the remedy.

How does this all begin? Spiritual bondages, whether addiction to alcohol, drugs, sexual perversity, or other negative behavior patterns are a consequence of the first act of defiance and unwillingness to obey a direct command of God for our protection. God said to Adam directly in Genesis 2: 16–17, "Of every tree of the garden you may freely eat, but of the tree of the knowledge of good and evil you shall not eat, for in the day that you eat of it you shall surely die" (NKJV). Rebellion against God's command in the early chapters of Genesis describes the fall of mankind and the corruption of God's perfect creative work. The result was and is physical and spiritual death in contrast to a once perfect harmony of body, mind, and spirit.

Beating the Odds of Negative Genes

Where is a good starting point to overcome the negative expressions of our physical, emotional, and spiritual genetic patterns? The first hope, of course, is accepting Jesus Christ and giving Him our all. Beating the odds of negative spiritual genetic patterns begins at this point. There may be some aspects of our physical, emotional, and spiritual genetic patterns that may be part of the past generations and not easily changed. In these cases, time and the experience of brokenness and God's supernatural healing is necessary. God is free, through the power of our commitment to His Son, to shape new attitudes, habits, and actions, and these changes can heal dysfunction that results from negative spiritual genetic patterns.

1. **Know God Firsthand**
   Living a wholesome life requires knowing God firsthand. If you are experiencing pain from the past and it seems that life is not currently a favorable experience, then I promise that if you get to know God firsthand you will have abundant joy and an abundant life. Jesus said in John 4:14, *"But whosoever drinketh of the water that I shall give him shall never thirst; but the water that I shall give him shall be in him a well of water springing up into everlasting life."* You will have no regrets as you allow God to shape your life and remove the old generational patterns of negative behavior. You will never thirst and will always be satisfied.

2. **Trust and Thank God for Abundant Life**

Nothing glorifies God more than our gratitude for the blessing of abundant life and peace. He is the only source of peace in a troubled world. The abundant life that God gives overcomes the world.

Francis Schaeffer, in his writings, outlines the alternatives that threaten the Christian. He states: "Overwhelming pressures are being brought to bear on people who have no absolutes, but only have the impoverished values of personal peace and prosperity. The pressures are progressively preparing modern people to accept a manipulative, authoritarian government. Unhappily many of these pressures are upon us now." Francis summarizes what affects the Christian in the pursuance of the abundant life of God.

- Economic breakdown: Ever-expanding affluence and economic breakdown
- War and/or serious threat of war: Pressures from other countries to conform and combine for a dominant authoritative government.
- Chaos of violence and terrorism: We have already seen how people give up liberties when they are faced with the threat of terrorism.
- Radical redistribution of the wealth of the world: A descending spiral of prosperity and world power can welcome an authoritarian government.
- A shortage of food, water, and other natural resources: This opens up movement to a reliance on human authoritarian means rather than God; a setup to accept a dominant authoritarianism.[12]

These threatening pressures that are upon us disturb our peace and create a stress that is progressive in nature. This environment initiates sickness and disease of various kinds to include sickness of the spirit, mind, and body.

3. **Live at Peace with God and Others**

   With the changes like the ones noted above taking place in our world, the impatience with others increases. The growing number of injustices and poor treatment of people from the unborn child to the elderly continues to desensitize people to the proper expression of love. An expression of godly love can only come from one that embraces the Master of life. Jesus taught us on many occasions that we are to love one another and, if possible, to live at peace with all men. The inner serenity of soul and spirit depends upon our ability to live at peace with God and others. In our interaction with other people we must treat them with care and compassion. We must forgive and move forward. We must learn to love the difficult while remaining strong in our faith and trust in God.

4. **Eat Wholesome and Nourishing Food**

   Junk food and a sick body are closely related. You are not going to get away with the Pepsi and Twinkie approach. Protein bars will not make you healthy either. Your body needs wholesome, nourishing food. Foods that are colorful and rich in vitamins and minerals are what the body and mind need for healthy balance. There are no quick fixes for a bad diet. Our current diet system is based upon what I call the SAD diet (Standard American Diet). Sad indeed! The Pepsi and Coke generation are dying off and have left this legacy to their offspring. I find it interesting that in our society we want to fix mistakes by further mistakes. Many of the current diets make the claim that you can eat what you want and still lose weight. This is a farce. If you eat bacon every day you're a heart attack in the making no matter what expert claims it as the best style of eating. The biblical way of eating can be summed up in one word—balance. We should also avoid foods that initiate unhealthy body function. Wholesome, healthy foods rich in color and fiber with the right balance of protein, carbohydrates, and essential fatty acids are necessary for a healthy body.

5. **God's Creative Beauty Contributes to Wholesome Views**
   God created the beauty of nature for our enjoyment and care, and it is available free of charge. The outdoors can restore and replenish our bodies, souls, and spirits. There are many studies that demonstrate that a walk in nature, which is full of beautiful greens, blues, reds, purples, and yellows, and the heat of the sun, calms and lifts our physical and emotional health and well-being. The healing balm of trees, oceans, mountains, and meadows are all here for our healing. John Muir, the renowned Alaskan explorer, basked in the beauty of it all and believed that it contributed greatly to the healing of his soul. How much more can God, coupled with the beauty of His creation, restore our souls and spirits?

6. **Take Time for Rest and Solitude**
   Our society fosters constant activity, and it is difficult to take a rest. But rest is absolutely essential. There must be some time away from the stresses of life. We all need a serene place and time to reflect and rest in God's care and comfort. In quietness and in confidence we are renewed to be more effective servants of God. Those who are weakened and pressured by this daily life will find rest in our Lord. *"Come unto me, all ye that are weak and heavy laden, and I will give you rest."* (Matt 11:28).

CHAPTER SEVEN

Healthy Lifestyle, Nourishment, and Daily Habits

"Each day we ought to renew our resolutions and arouse ourselves to fervor as though it were the first day of our religious life. We ought to say: 'Help me, O Lord God, in my good resolution and in Your holy service. Grant me now, this very day, to begin perfectly, for thus far I have done nothing.' It is characteristic of a humble soul always to do good and to think little of itself. It is a mark of great purity and deep faith to look for no consolation in created things. The man who desires no justification from without has clearly entrusted himself to God: 'For not he who commendeth himself is approved,' says St. Paul, 'but he whom God commendeth.'"[13]

What Constitutes a Healthy Lifestyle?

There is no substitute for clean living. My pastor affirms this in his preaching. I'm glad he reminds me of this because it keeps fresh in my mind the importance of making right choices that guide me and my family in the things of God, and also reminds me that God is pleased by my good life choices. How do you break an old bad habit? Well, contrary to what you may have heard, it is not as simple as developing a new, clean habit.

89

Many times individuals have told me that they can end an addiction by just deciding to stop. Most of the individuals who take this position are still addicted to drugs, nicotine, alcohol, sex, gambling, and other worldly habits. It is not as simple as saying, "I can stop whenever I want to."

Your lifestyle is a determining factor in how healthy you remain. Individuals working seventy hours per week are not practicing wholesome lifestyles. Partying hard doesn't constitute a healthy lifestyle, even though it feels like a good time. Anything that drives or harms the body and decreases the soul and spiritual senses to God and the creation that He has blessed us with is a harmful practice. God's lifestyle design is:

- Devotion to and worship of God first
- Continual development of wholesome life habits
- Commitment and loyalty to spouse
- Commitment and loyalty to family
- Commitment and service in church-related activities
- Commitment and service to employer
- Commitment and service to neighbors and community

In order for us to honor these commitments, we must have adequate rest and relaxation. Got wants us to take advantage of the rest that He provides for our total health and wellbeing. He has also provided nature for our nurture. We are not just an assortment of physical genes with a predetermined set of risks and benefits with no need for the beautiful environment that God has created for our rest and relaxation. Even the typical scientific mind that makes no room for God and assesses every life event in terms of methodology and deduction, affirms that our genes allow us to learn, imitate, imprint, and express instincts. The nature versus nurture argument scientifically states: *"It is genes that allow the human mind to learn, to remember, to imitate, to imprint, to absorb culture, and to express instincts.*"[14] The inquiring mind and the intellect are impressed by genetic determination because it is a mystery that needs a continual unraveling, and there is something scintillating about this. However, the mystery of it is cloaked in the genius of God, the genome of God, the high intellect of God, the omnipotence and omniscience of God. It seems to me that there is more weight on this platform than just the mere unraveling of a mystery and some mathematical formula to rationalize away what God has formed from the elements found in the universe. Nature versus nurture should rightfully be a nature and nurture alliance designed by God to complete His creative work.

Nourishment of Spirit, Soul, and Body

The balance of nourishment is not just based upon what the body needs or the genetic makeup of the organism; it is what the whole person needs. There must be nurture for the entire being, which includes the three parts that make the whole spirit, soul, and body.

Nourishment is that which promotes growth in any way. It's not just about food. Healthy, wholesome food for nourishment is essential. It is important to have colorful, flavorful foods in our diet. This diet should contain a variety of green vegetables and bitter greens, fresh fruit, adequate fiber, good fats, water, and a balance of protein and complex carbohydrates. Adequate amounts of each are required for balance. Eating for nourishment and health are the right reasons for eating and helps maintain a healthy body. Eating to relieve stress or for comfort is not God's design for food. Overeating and undernourishment are also displeasing to God, because it is a self-destructive pattern. God is not glorified if food is the ruling force and determining agent in our comfort and pleasure. God should be the only source of all of our comfort, not food. Food is for nourishment, and we can enjoy a good meal. God wants us to enjoy food, but to dote on it borders on gluttony and is offensive to God. Gluttonous behavior in regard to food is displeasing to God the same as other addictions or compulsive behaviors.

Balance is very important as it relates to feeding our souls. What you feed into your mind can form and cultivate a habit. An old Indian saying is *bad thought, bad habit*. This is simple but true. If you plant questionable thoughts in your mind, your behavior will reflect bad habits. If you feed your mind pornography, your habits will reflect that focus. Hateful thoughts toward your neighbor will eventually manifest as bursts of anger toward individuals. Forsaking God in your thought life leads to apostasy and hopelessness for eternity. Feed on God and live with joy. The blessing of the Lord makes a person rich in soul and spirit, and there is no sorrow or regret associated with it.

The spirit needs quiet and rest in order to grow and develop. The Scripture that tells us to be still and know God is a direct example of spirit nurture. Elijah had to be still by the brook, Moses had to be still in Midian, David had to be still in the caves, Joseph had to be still in prison, Daniel and his three friends had to be still in the fiery furnace, Paul had to be still on the Damascus road, and John had to be still on Patmos. It is necessary for all to have the still, quiet instruction of the spirit, a direct nurture of the Holy Spirit. The spirit needs a direct connection to God in order to be filled with vitality and fervor. There is no other source for spirit nurture. Any other source is damaging and potentially a threat to the safety and nurture of your spirit.

What Can I Do to Build My Spirit and Soul?

- Feed on God's Word by reading and meditating daily.

- Pray in faith, believing God is active at every turn whether or not you can see, feel, or touch Him.
- Focus upon resources that graft God's attributes upon the spirit and soul.
- Prayer, reflection, and introspection are necessary for inventory and works that create this space are helpful.
- Read good, moral works of great servants of God.
- Read biographical works that reflect life lessons in faith, determination, courage, and service.
- Have regular quiet retreats to collect your thoughts and feed your spirit.
- Ask the Holy Spirit to fill your spirit and soul with vitality, fervor, and joy.

Our habits reflect our thoughts. A habit is a tendency toward an action or condition, which by repetition has become spontaneous. What are your spontaneous actions? Some individuals have bad habits that they feel they can break at any time, but they allow them to persist. Old habits can be hard to break. However, God works the impossible with those who cooperate. We can break bad habits and develop healthy new habits by the grace and strength of the Lord. It all depends upon how seriously we take it. I like chocolate, but if I am allergic to it, I had better stay away from chocolate or it can become a problem. If smoking and drinking alcohol are killing you, don't you think it is time to break the habit? If gluttony has become a problem, then don't you think it is time to ask God to balance your appetite and develop healthy eating habits? If pornography is a problem, don't you believe it's time to look at something that builds a healthy respect of self instead of degrading and disgustingly filthy acts that diminish self-respect and sear the spirit and soul? What is put into the mind can either build up or tear down the spirit. The reverse is true also. Evil is prevalent in our world. You don't have to go looking for it, for it will find its way to you. The Bible states: *"There hath no temptation taken you but such as is common to man: but God is faithful, who will not suffer you to be tempted above that ye are able; but will with the temptation also make a way, to escape, that ye may be able to bear it"* (1 Corinthians 10:13).

CHAPTER EIGHT

Harmony and Balance of Fight and Rest

"The body is one unit, though it is made up of many cells and though all the cells are many, they form one body."

(Dr. Paul Brand)

Triple Fs and Triple Rs

The delicate balance between fight and rest must be understood in order to obtain total health. The pace at which our world moves easily upsets the balance between work and play, busyness and rest, noise and quietness. God created the body as a series of systems that work in harmony to keep a healthy function and balance. The Bible explicitly states that the body of mankind was formed from the dust of the ground. The Hebrew word for man, *adam*, derives directly from the Hebrew word *adamah*, meaning ground or soil. The difference in all of creation in the creative work is that mankind is created as a living soul, a complete higher creation of God. One of the most fascinating systems that demonstrates this is our stress adaptation response. There are two key systems: the sympathetic (FFF) and parasympathetic (RRR).

- **Fight, Flight, and Fright (FFF)**
When we are running in the adrenalin mode with our pedal to the metal all the time, the light will eventually dim and burn out. Imagine always operating in a mode that requires continual adrenalin. I like to explain it in terms of bracing yourself for the biggest car wreck ever. Have you ever had a near-miss accident where your heart was in your mouth and you experienced the feeling that is only encountered in fight, flight, and fright experiences? Yes, God created this for a reason—to protect from impending trauma or harm. The nervous system regulates this activity, and it is called a sympathetic response. There are many individuals who operate in a sympathetic mode most of the time. These individuals are aggressive personality types who are always on the move, pursuing the next big thing and forgetting the most beautiful aspects of God's intended rest. Virtually all of the human body is affected by this system. When it is out of balance it contributes to the wear and tear process physically, emotionally, and spiritually. The positive aspects of the triple Fs are that they can protect from trauma and harm and keep the balance of positive motivation and energy when appropriately balanced the way God intends with rest, repose, and relaxation.

- **Rest, Repose, and Relaxation (RRR)**
Why is the concept of rest and relaxation so difficult to grasp? Our world communicates in an entirely different fashion than it did during the Twentieth Century. I read a perfect example of this recently in an article published by *Scientific American* entitled "The Science of Persuasion."

Social psychology has determined the basic principles that govern our responses. The article discusses six persuasive principles responsible for why we say yes and have difficulty resisting a sales ploy. This system is in place in the business world and is a significant life experience for most people. These six principles are: reciprocation, consistency, social validation, liking, authority, and scarcity—all of which are geared toward activating our sympathetic system and keeping it continuously active. The bottom line of this system is, *if everyone's doing it, why shouldn't I?*[15] There must be a parasympathetic balance, and the only way to get it is to have peaceful surroundings, good wholesome lighting from the sun and green spectrum from nature, relaxing baths, massage, wholesome food and conversation, good fellowship with friends, and most of all, a meditative and prayerful time of quietness every day with God.

I often hear from well-meaning businesspersons in the corporate world about the promise of wealth and financial security with an incredible amount of time off. However, as I observe individuals consumed by this approach, I notice that they are always engaged in the triple F mode with no rest factored in. Most don't even realize how consumed they really are. I know, because I have been there many times and have purposed to factor in the triple Rs. It is not a bad thing to be engaged in life with the excitement of making a great living in a career that brings enjoyment. However, if we do not get the rest needed, our candle dims and our vitality suffers. Rest, repose, and relaxation don't just happen. They are in extreme competition with the triple Fs. Planning is the key to activating the triple Rs. You need to rest for several days at a time. Some may not have the luxury of doing this right now. However, if a plan is developed, there will be more rest and relaxation experienced because it will not be neglected. For example, many people I have talked with over the years haven't sat down with a good book in a quiet place or taken a family trip away from business in a long time. There is something wrong in this picture. You need peace and quiet on a regular basis, and if you do not get it, your candle dims. Planning is the key to rest, repose, and relaxation.

Our Hormonal System

- **The Brain**

  As we explore the amazingly complex systems of the body we find that the main control center is the brain. We use a very small portion of our brains on a daily basis. God has created an amazingly complex multitasking center that is faster than any existing computing system on the face of the planet. The human brain, as created by God, is a higher function center than that of any existing animal. God has created man with intelligence and the ability to reason. No other living thing on the face of this planet can do this. The human brain is a complex center of circuitry that controls many different activities, ranging from the ability to move limbs to sensory actions of smell, taste, touch, sight, and hearing. All of these crucial functions that assist us every day are working in harmony. The brain is the main center that sends messages to the systems whether chemical, electrical, or mechanical. It is amazing that many processes including the light-dark cycle and temperature and electromagnetic impulses are all vital parts in transmitting signals in the body. Balance depends upon total integration of all systems.

- **Stressors and the Alarm Response**

  Sympathetic and parasympathetic nervous interaction and the secretion of certain hormones in stress determine our body's response, namely epinephrine, norepinephrine, cortisol, and biochemical messengers. Epinephrine, also known as adrenalin, is the biochemical messenger that is secreted when the triple F system is activated. This is also known as the sympathetic response. Norepinephrine, also known as noradrenalin, is secreted to help counterbalance the effects of adrenalin. The triple R system is responsible for this activity, also known as the parasympathetic response. These systems must work in unison to keep balance and to allow the body to adapt to the stressors that are encountered.

  In our bodies the foundational material for all hormones is something probably familiar to you. It is called *cholesterol*, and when the body is in an increased stress environment—internally or externally—more cholesterol is made. From cholesterol comes another crucial hormone called cortisol. Cortisol is the body's natural steroid that is made in response to stress. Cortisol regulates the immune system, helps the body respond to stress, regulates fat metabolism, and has other crucial functions. The human body is on a twenty-four hour time clock called a circadian rhythm. Cortisol is secreted over a twenty-four hour period and is supposed to have its higher levels in the morning hours to adjust for the demands of the day. It is supposed to be lower as the body unwinds to prepare for rest.

  When the stressors are more than the body can bear, or when the protective factors begin to fail (the body's ability to adapt to the stressor), fatigue and loss of stamina result. If this occurs without any hope of some change and nurture, collapse can result (burn out). Prolonged stress can lead to distress and cause adrenal fatigue (the glands responsible in regulating stress) and total collapse in severe cases. It should also be noted that the body suppresses its natural immunity as the cortisol levels rise and stay elevated. Did you ever question the reason you develop a cold or virus? It is because of the body's let-down after prolonged stress. The secretion of cortisol is responsible. When you put cortisone cream on a rash, what does it do? The rash diminishes and clears up with continued use. Why? It suppresses the immune reaction to whatever is aggravating the area, and it inhibits inflammation. This is the same action cortisol has in the body. Prolonged high levels of stress can cause excessive secretion of cortisol and suppresses the body's natural immune response. While running in the adrenalin mode, the body is numb to this. It's when the stress is suddenly reduced or removed while at rest that the body down-regulates and becomes susceptible to illness and infection.

I mentioned two key parts of the nervous system—the sympathetic and parasympathetic systems. The sympathetic is also known as the *fight, flight, and fright system*, and the parasympathetic is the *rest, repose, and relax system*. The purpose of the two systems is to keep a balance. The sympathetic system prepares us to respond to stress and emergencies. However, if it is activated continuously, it leads to a fatigued state. The parasympathetic system is active when the body is in a relaxed state and is vital in counterbalancing the sympathetic system as well as its own independent functions. The chart below summarizes our discussion:

Sympathetic (Fight, Flight, Fright)	Parasympathetic (Rest, Repose, Relax)
Alarm reaction to protect in stress and trauma (increased cortisol and lipids)	Down regulating of alarm reaction (balanced cortisol)
Constriction of vessels and diverting of blood flow (can lead to angina)	Restoring of blood flow and vessel tone
Activation of the shock mechanisms (drop in pressure + body temperature)	Activation of relaxation mechanisms (normal pressure + body temperature)

There are ways to balance the alarm response. The most essential are rest, a diversion away from the stress routine, nature (the green color of nature activates the calming pathways), prayer and meditation with God, supportive friendships, adequate nutrition and replacement of certain nutrients, peaceful meal settings, adequate intake of water, reframing your view of life, your mission and purpose (seeing everything from God's frame of reference), and surrendering all of your persisting cares in this life. It's hard, I know, but it is possible. There will be new challenges and obstacles that will test this new discipline, but you should discover that the anxieties of the day are given over more quickly each time. It is a life lesson and not an instantaneous acquiring of coping strategies that are not always reliable for the types of tests that may come our way. The dependence is upon God to meet the stress and provide the grace and grit through the process.

Our Hearts and Circulation

- **Stressors and Damaged Heart and Vessels**
  The heart and vessels are important parts of the body that carry blood and nutrients to the rest of the systems that depend upon them for nurture. The heart is a pump that God created to work to pump the life force of blood through the network of sophisticated tubing that at one point is so narrow that only one red cell at a time can pass through. The intricate vessels of the eye are so tiny and crucial to sight that if they were narrowed or blocked, the delicate sense of vision could be lost.

  Negative stresses can adversely affect the health of the heart and vessels. Prolonged internal stress, whether from poor dietary and lifestyle factors, or external stress caused by traumatic events, illness, and other factors, are shown to increase what is called free radical disease. Free radical disease accelerates plaque development in the arterial system and can seriously damage the heart. Pay attention to the warning flags of increased negative stress.

INTERNAL WARNING FLAGS

Increased Cholesterol (Lipids)

HDL lowers (not good).

LDL increases (not good).

Increased Blood Pressure

Increased risk of stroke of heart.

Vascular resistance and obstruction.

Increased Homocysteine

Increased abrasive action on vessels and scarring, the result of accelerated free radical disease.

Increased Inflammatory Proteins

Common protein secreted when injury results. Inflammatory proteins are genetically controlled, therefore a good genetic indicator of risk (known as (C-Reactive Protein).

Our Natural Immunity

The whole purpose of the immune system is to ensure the safety of friend and protect against foe. Prolonged stress with no rest can inhibit immunity. Our physical genes, which are found on our chromosomes, help to determine the code and sequence necessary to identify friend or foe. However, the environment and numerous physical, emotional, and spiritual stressors can impair immunity against disease despite good genes.

The immune system is made up of several components that help defend against invaders that gain entrance into the body. The immune system is broken down into cellular defenses and overall body defenses. There is an entire cascade of events that are well integrated to systematically identify and eradicate an invader. The immune system is continuously challenged by familiar, strange, and odd foreign substances that can include environmental agents, viruses, bacteria, parasites, foreign antigens, toxic drug remnants (antibiotics and other cell and system toxic drugs), and internal processes that for some reason go out of control. The immune system must continually update its information systems when defending against disease-causing agents that are stealthy (able to evade detection). Immune defense includes an intact genetic signaling, immune complement cascade, white blood cells (specific types), antibodies, and other components that we are not completely familiar with at this time. All of these components work together for total body defense.

Our spiritual immunity is very similar to our physical immunity. There are dark forces that can break down our spiritual defenses. Our spiritual genes, created by God, are encoded for our spiritual defenses. Our spiritual defense is faith in Jesus as Savior, an unwavering trust in God's Word, an active discernment of spiritual dangers, an identification of spiritual weaknesses and strengths in the family generations, and a constant and active prayer commitment. All of this is integrated for a thorough protection from the evils in our world today, and continual updating is necessary for complete protection!

Our Defenses

Just as the body's defenses are active continuously, so must spiritual defenses be active continuously. A breakdown in body defense facilitates illness or disease that can result in sickness. A breakdown of soul and spiritual defense can result in depression, anxiety, loss of hope, and ultimately self-destruction. There must be an active engagement with God. He understands life's troubling events and provides answers and hope for them all. There is an amazing similarity to how our physical body responds against the harm of potential invaders and how our spiritual defenses respond against dark forces of evil. Briefly, there are two main components of our physical immunity against harmful agents like bacteria, viruses, parasites, and foreign agents. These two systems are essential in human survival and adaptation to a potentially threatening environment. Similarly, there are two systems essential in defense against the unseen forces present in our world that can inflict harm.

The Arms of the Physical Immune System

1. Cellular Defense: Direct intervention on a cellular level happens when an identified invader tries to gain entry into the living cell. An amazing sequence of events occurs as the immune system identifies and destroys the invader, which leads to total destruction of the infected cell to prevent further infection.

2. System Defense: A total body surveillance force in identifying and destroying invaders like virus, bacteria, and other microbial forces similar to what is done when ground forces in the military close in on an enemy and use precision firing to destroy the threat. These two systems work in unison to assure complete immune defense against potentially damaging forces. At the same time the body regenerates new cells to restore function and make provisions for the loss experienced by the invasion process.

The Spiritual Immune System

Just as in our physical immune defense, our spiritual genes give the code and sequence to identify friend or foe to assure a right relationship with God and the people around us and to defend against spiritual invaders. Our spiritual immune system has the following defenses.

1. Repentance: Before there can be spiritual immunity there must be a complete turning away from old destructive patterns. The only way this can be achieved is by coming to Jesus with no reservations and allowing Him to take away the darkness and replace it all with His light and life. Ask

this Friend to be the Lord of all. The triple Rs are made possible by the right foundation of repentance.

2. Faith: A complete and total reliance upon God for all sustenance by a personal, active, and living experience with Jesus. This experience, integrated into the human spirit and carried out through the human soul, includes the expression of the mind, human will, and expression of emotion. The anxiety produced over the triple Fs of life and the resolution of them is made possible by faith.

3. Prayer: A continuous surveillance and identification of physical, emotional, and spiritual needs and an active request for provision of these needs through divine intervention and human action. In addition, prayer enables an active identification of potential dangers from external and internal sources and through a direct communication link with the Creator of all mankind.

These defenses are necessary for complete surveillance and action to be intact. Repentance, faith, and prayer are the first-line defenders against troubles that affect the human soul and spirit that are similar to the cellular arm, the first defense for the physical body. What the cell defenses cannot achieve, the system defenses will. Both work in unison to keep our physical bodies fighting off agents that can harm us. Repentance allows for the relationship to be started with God in the driver's seat. Faith and prayer work together to touch the throne of God and liberate the power of God to defend against dark forces that could harm the soul and spirit.

His Blood and Our Blood

There is a saying, "The life is in the blood." When we discuss immune health, the blood is one of the essential components involved in the defense strategy of the human body. Dr. Paul Brand talks about the blood cells as an amazing life force that serves specific functions. More particularly, he tells us:

> "More interesting are the white blood cells, that armed forces of the body which guard against invaders—sometimes they creep along the veins and sometimes free-floating in the bloodstream—When they arrive the battle begins."[16]

Jesus said, "Drink it, all of you, this is my blood . . ." (Matthew 26:27–28). This was a very powerful statement from our Lord. Think about what He was referring to when He said, "Drink of it." Jesus was talking about infusing His life into us. Blood represents life, and the Old Testament shows us that drinking blood is considered unclean. Jesus was not talking about the act of drinking blood. He was talking about consuming His lifeblood that never dies. He was talking about a life that shares in the sacrifice that assures the living hope of eternity. The lifeblood of Jesus gives the foundational elements of our peaceful and hopeful existence on the planet despite the devastating stressors of life!

Our Digestion and Detoxification

- **Peace and a good meal**
  A peaceful meal settles the spirit and satisfies the soul. There are many digestive functions that are regulated by our nervous system to assure a healthy balance. Stress during mealtime is common. Many business lunches are spent discussing stressful topics. I was recently in a café and overheard a performance evaluation being discussed with the recipient of the evaluation subjected to knowing that diners at the surrounding tables could hear every word. This was neither the time nor the place for such critique. Don't

accept business lunches. A business meeting should remain a business meeting, and a meal with colleagues or friends should remain a meal. I recently heard a story of a man who retired from his job after thirty-five years. He had been an executive and had attended many business lunches. Those lunches were used to discuss future projects and other business topics. During his first month of retirement, he tried setting lunch dates with his former lunch companions and discovered that they had no time for him. He was no longer part of their business crowd. This caused him to reflect on the differences between colleagues and friends. There are different types of friendships: casual friends, positional friends, personal friends, and intimate friends. Intimate friendships are rare, and you can probably count them on your hand. These are the friends who know your heart and have been loyal through thick and thin. Positional friendships are established in the work environment and, as mentioned above, are dependent solely on the work environment. Casual friendships are usually "*Hi, how are you?*" and "*Goodbye.*" Personal friends are not the same as intimate friends, as you see them more frequently and share more of your life with them, but not on the same level as intimate friends. What does this have to do with digestion? Sit and have a meal with people you can stomach, because you will have indigestion if you keep company with contentious people.

The digestive system is an amazingly complex interaction of fine functions coordinated perfectly to use nutrients and burn energy (calories) from food. This is where we get our energy for everyday use. The digestive tract is a hollow tube from mouth to anus and between these two points there are processes known as digestion, absorption, and metabolism taking place. What comes into the body via the mouth does in fact play an important role in our total health and well-being. In the colon we find the utilization of water, the manufacturing of vitamins and other fatty acids vital to health, mineral metabolism and fiber usage to push things along and facilitate waste removal and the purging. At the same time there is a fine ecological balance of good bacteria versus bad bacteria. Make it a point to have your meals in a peaceful setting, choose good company during meals, eat wholesome food, and be sure that while on any medication that depletes the delicate balance of the bowel—such as antibiotics—that you replace the friendly bacteria with probiotics like acidophilus.

- **Human Emotions and the Process of Digestion**
  The human emotions of joy, contentment, love, and peace are settling to the gut. There are many *gut people* walking around out there. In other words, the immediate negative emotions and stressors are taken to the weakest point and for some that may be the gut. For others it may be the lungs, and for others the heart, and so on. Negative emotions do alter the digestive function and the delicate balance in the bowel. These emotions of anger, bitterness, envy, and hatred cause everything to stay knotted. When this is a prolonged experience, serious diseases can result. The most severe of these is cancer. It is so important to change old habits of allowing negative emotions to remain and instead give them over to God and accept His forgiveness, love, joy, and peace. In summary, the types of foods eaten are essential to health, the types of relationships we have are essential to health, the types of emotions we retain are essential to health, and most important of all—what we do with God's overtures will determine our level of acceptance, love, peace, joy, and eternal hope.

- **Innate Cleaning, Preserving, and Fasting**
  The Bible is clear on the concept of fasting. The human body automatically moves into a detoxification mode when the toxic load is high. There is an appointed time to fast, and not everyone can do it the same way. There may be some restrictions that would require a modified, supervised fast. Individuals with blood sugar problems, chronic illness, and frail metabolism must be supervised. It is not prudent to initiate a fast without accountability. I have heard of individuals doing extended fasts. Some made it through the fasting process fine and others were sickened by the increased toxic load in the body. Liver and bowel detoxification are good things to do occasionally; my suggestion is that you consult your health care practitioner in order to do this safely.

  The prime reason to fast is to draw closer in spirit and soul to God. The spiritual senses are sharpened and our spiritual ears are better able to discern what God is saying to us. There is an appointed time to fast, and you should seek God's will and then be accountable to someone during the process. Also, let your physician in on what you are doing. He or she may be able to give some helpful suggestions. A chosen fast should be a prayerful fast. The fasting should not be exclusively used for detoxification of the body. It must also be used in the cleansing of the soul and spirit from the toxic forces of this world in exchange for the holiness and purity of God.

- **Taking Things to the Gut**
  There are a number of factors that can affect our digestive process. Some of these include:

  - Stress and anxiety

110

- Poor diet
- Excessive antibiotic use
- Heavy metal toxicity
- Environmental exposure
- Bacterial and viral infection

There are many symptoms that can be experienced by a faulty digestive process and some of these include:

- Acid Reflux
- Headache
- Joint and muscle aching
- Fatigue
- Energy loss
- Water retention

There are conditions known as irritable bowel syndrome (spastic colon) and leaky gut syndrome that can be caused by a combination of irritants including fear, worry, anxiety, and poor lifestyle habits. Studies indicate that only twenty percent of the U.S. population experiences functionally intact bowel health. Bowel immunity is drastically reduced by poor health habits. In order for restoration to occur, there must be the right balance of nutrients, rest, relaxation, and focus on the use of healing agents that will promote bowel healing. Leaky gut occurs when the natural protective membrane barrier of the bowel is damaged by a constant assault of some or all of the above listed irritants. The gap spaces between the intestinal cells widen and allow large matter to pass through the barrier; in individuals with normal bowel function this is not the case. There are a number of things that can help the bowel to heal, but such a discussion is too extensive to cover here. I mention it only to demonstrate how the body as a whole can be affected by continuous fight, flight, and fright without adequate rest. When the stress level is high, cortisol activity is also high. Remember, this is a natural hormone produced by the body to respond to high stress. When this cortisol is secreted excessively it suppresses immune function and leaves the bowel vulnerable to poor defense and inflammation. It is important to not let it go this far. Identify the factors that may have a negative effect and take the steps necessary for prevention or healing. Eliminate the causative agents, eat a good diet, eliminate negative stressors, replace nutrients that will assist in healing the bowel and detoxifying the body and learn to *rest*. However, the most important step to take is to give all of your fears, anxieties, worries, and weaknesses to Jesus, who can give you a settling peace.

CHAPTER NINE

Miraculous and Mysterious Healings of Jesus

"And Jesus went about all Galilee, teaching in their synagogues, and preaching the gospel of the kingdom, and healing all manner of sickness and all manner of disease among the people."
(Matthew 4:23)

"Having walked with Him now for over fifty years, I've finally worked up the courage to say it publicly, loud and clear: God's will—from our finite, human standpoint—is a mystery. That's right, M-Y-S-T-E-R-Y."
(Charles Swindoll)

Jesus Heals the Multitudes

"And they that were vexed with unclean spirits: and they were healed. And the whole multitude sought to touch him: for there went virtue out of him, and healed them all."
(Luke 6:18–19)

Jesus was moved with compassion when He met people who suffered burdens, physical illnesses, and spiritual and emotional heaviness. Jesus sensed their needs and knew

113

the deeper, underlying causes for their pain and illnesses. The significance of healing the multitude was to demonstrate that the power of God was personal, powerful, and effective. He wanted all to know that God met personal needs and that through His mercy, love, and forgiveness healing is extended.

Jesus performed personal miracles that met heart and spirit needs. The foundational teaching is *personal faith, trust,* and *obedience* in the will of God and the promises of God. Can you imagine the demands that were placed upon our Lord? He experienced the pains and afflictions. He was familiar with grief and suffering. He knew the power of the dark forces present in this world that could control and lead to total hopelessness. He came to die for the sin of mankind—sin that leads to brokenness. He heals the broken hearted. He gives sight to the blind and opens deaf ears to His message in order to free mankind from sin. He healed all manner of disease; He liberated souls from oppression, and offered eternal peace and joy. He is the complete remedy for the human condition.

And the best news is that healing that comes from the power and presence of the Holy Spirit is here for us today, still active and effective. Man does not heal. God heals. Exercise your faith in the will and care of God, trust Him, and He will perform His promise to you. Do not hold back; believe in His healing work and live fully for Jesus.

The Centurion's Servant

"And when Jesus was entered into Capernaum, there came unto him a centurion, beseeching him, And saying, Lord, my servant lieth at home sick of the palsy, grievously tormented. And Jesus saith unto him, I will come and heal him. The centurion answered and said, Lord, I am not worthy that thou shouldest come under my roof: but speak the word only, and my servant shall be healed. For I am a

man under authority, having soldiers under me: and I say to this man, Go, and he goeth; and to another, Come, and he cometh; and my servant, Do this, and he doeth it. When Jesus heard it, he marvelled, and said to them that followed, Verily I say unto you, I have not found so great faith, no, not in Israel. And I say unto you, That many shall come from the east and west, and shall sit down with Abraham, and Isaac, and Jacob, in the kingdom of heaven. But the children of the kingdom shall be cast out into outer darkness: there shall be weeping and gnashing of teeth. And Jesus said unto the centurion, Go thy way; and as thou hast believed, so be it done unto thee. And his servant was healed in the selfsame hour."

(Matt. 8:5–13)

This is a fascinating account of a man of authority, a Roman commander. This man immediately recognized Jesus as Lord and Master. He was looking out for his servant; he had compassion and humility, and Jesus recognized this immediately. He did not invite Jesus into his house because he knew that Jesus was God in the flesh. He knew only Jesus could perform the miracle for his servant. The centurion was humble and spiritually ready to receive. Jesus said He would come and heal, and He did. The centurion said, "Just speak the word Lord. You don't have to come, for I am not worthy to receive You." Jesus proclaimed that He had not seen such a great faith in all of Israel. Imagine, "among Israel" faith was sorely lacking; the doubt factor was high. In fact, there was a deliberate plot to stop what Jesus was called by His Father to do, to heal the broken hearted, to deliver the oppressed, to set the captives free, to give sight to the blind, to die for all humanity, and rise from death to life to establish the eternal hope in glory. As it was with the centurion, so it is with us. We must possess the great faith and affirm within that we are not worthy to receive Him but have faith that if we speak the word, we will be healed.

Jairus's Daughter and the Woman Who Touched Jesus (Faith Versus Fear)

"And it came to pass, that, when Jesus was returned, the people gladly received him: for they were all waiting for him. And, behold, there came a man named Jairus, and he was a ruler of the synagogue: and he fell down at Jesus' feet, and besought him that he would come into his house: For he had one only daughter, about twelve years of age, and she lay dying. But as he went the people thronged him. And a woman having an issue of blood twelve years, which had spent all her living upon physicians, neither could be healed of any, Came behind him, and touched the border of his garment: and immediately her issue of blood stanched. And Jesus said, Who touched me? When all denied, Peter and they that were with him said, Master, the multitude throng thee and press thee, and sayest thou, Who touched me? And Jesus said, Somebody hath touched me: for I perceive that virtue is gone out of me. And when the woman saw that she was not hid, she came trembling, and falling down before him, she declared unto him before all the people for what cause she had touched him, and how she was healed immediately. And he said unto her, Daughter, be of good comfort: thy faith hath made thee whole; go in peace. While he yet spake, there cometh one from the ruler of the synagogue's house, saying to him, Thy daughter is dead; trouble not the Master. But when Jesus heard it, he answered him, saying, Fear not: believe only, and she shall be made whole. And when he came into the house, he suffered no man to go in, save Peter, and James, and John, and the father and the mother of the maiden. And all wept, and bewailed her: but he said, Weep not; she is not dead, but sleepeth. And they laughed him to scorn, knowing that she was dead. And he put them all out, and took her by the hand, and called, saying, Maid, arise. And her spirit came again, and she arose straightway: and he commanded to give her meat. And her parents were astonished."

(Luke 8:40–56)

This healing clearly demonstrates faith in action and fear as a detriment. As in the Roman Centurion's account, the woman with the issue of blood reached out in faith. Jesus met her need to demonstrate the emphasis that He places on faith. Jairus's first response was to fear, which is a natural human response. The needs of these individuals were extreme, and Jesus, from the very beginning of the events, intended to heal because of His great love and compassion. However, He did delay. Jairus invited Jesus to come to his house, a sharp contrast to the Roman Centurion's response, saying that he was not worthy for Jesus to come under his roof. The healing power of Jesus was active, but the circumstances seemed so complex.

Let's look at these complex events. There was a woman in the crowd while the petition of Jairus came forth. Jesus responded immediately to the woman who had anguish of soul and spirit and reached out in faith and believed that if she could touch the Master, she would be healed. She was. Jesus then proclaimed that it was her faith that made her whole. She worshipped Jesus and trusted Him to work the miracle of healing. She wasn't seeking the miracle alone; she was seeking the life answer, the eternal hope and peace. There was no other solution—she tried them all. She retained the services of many physicians and was helped by none of them! Jesus healed her and proclaimed it accomplished by her faith.

In Jairus's daughter's case Jesus delayed his coming, and the reason is revealed when Jesus said to all present, "Fear not." Faith was not the prime catalyst of this miracle as it was in the woman who touched Jesus. Jairus's daughter had died and all were told not to trouble the Master. Jesus moved to where the girl was and told her family and friends that she was only sleeping. They laughed at Him with *scorn*. This strong word means *derision*, and the Lord healed the girl anyway. He called them all out, took her by the hand, told her to arise, and her spirit came alive. He told her to eat, and she did; her parents were astonished. Jesus didn't affirm to any in the household that faith was the basis for this healing experience. No one had demonstrated faith. Astonishment is not the same as faith. Being astonished at the miracle is human. Faith in Jesus is the miracle worker. What He requires is a ready heart, a burdened soul, and a spirit ready for transformation. The household of Jairus had none of these. Jesus worked the miracle anyway because of His compassion and the life lesson it teaches. Faith brings the hope of eternal joy. Physical healing is temporary, but spiritual healing is eternal.

The day the woman with the bleeding disorder experienced the healing work of Jesus she was made completely whole. The greatest healing that took place that day was that her spirit became one with Jesus. The dead were made alive by the hand of Jesus; in order to stay alive, a living and active faith must be present. Fear inhibits faith and clutters and confuses life. Jesus broke through all the confusion when He ordered those at Jairus's house to leave. Their fear and unbelief could not be present because it would hinder the work of God. Don't allow the distraction of fear to consume you. It's hard to overcome fear, but it's necessary to obtain a greater dimension of faith. Reach out in faith and touch the garment of Jesus and be healed.

Nobleman's Son Healed

"And there was a certain nobleman, whose son was sick at Capernaum. When he heard that Jesus was come out of Judaea into Galilee, he went unto him, and besought him that he would come down, and heal his son: for he was at the point of death. Then said Jesus unto him, Except ye see signs and wonders, ye will not believe. The nobleman saith unto him, Sir, come down ere my child die. Jesus saith unto him, Go thy way; thy son liveth. And the man believed the word that Jesus had spoken unto him, and he went his way. And as he was now going down, his servants met him, and told him, saying, Thy son liveth. Then enquired he of them the hour when he began to amend. And they said unto him, Yesterday at the seventh hour the fever left him. So the father knew that it was at the

same hour, in which Jesus said unto him, Thy son liveth: and him-
self believed, and his whole house."

(John 4:46–53)

What do you know! The miracle worker is in town. The human heart seeks signs and wonders. The beliefs upon the signs are
based on the performance of the miracle. Jesus recognized the signs
and knew the motives of the heart. How difficult it must have been
at times. He reached out and in all cases wanted the best for all
who experienced healing in one form or another. However, in this
case, the nobleman was seeking a miracle. Jesus understood this
man's need for the physical manifestation of God's power. The man
believed the words of Jesus, and from that instant Jesus said, "Go
thy way; thy son liveth." His son was well; the result demonstrated
the power of God to work at a distance. Everyone in this man's
household believed because of it.

Did you ever pray for someone far away who was stricken with
an illness, and you felt powerless to do anything? When we are
faithfully reminded to pray, God performs the miracle from a distance. Time and distance are not obstacles in God's day or hour. If
there are any restrictions, they are not coming from God unless He
wills things to be delayed. I am learning that God is not bound by
the ordinary. He performs the extraordinary.

Jesus Heals the Lame Man

"After this there was a feast of the Jews; and Jesus went up to Jerusa-
lem. Now there is at Jerusalem by the sheep market a pool, which is
called in the Hebrew tongue Bethesda, having five porches. In these
lay a great multitude of impotent folk, of blind, halt, withered, wait-
ing for the moving of the water. For an angel went down at a certain
season into the pool, and troubled the water: whosoever then first
after the troubling of the water stepped in was made whole of what-
soever disease he had. And a certain man was there, which had an

119

infirmity thirty and eight years. When Jesus saw him lie, and knew that he had been now a long time in that case, he saith unto him, Wilt thou be made whole? The impotent man answered him, Sir, I have no man, when the water is troubled, to put me into the pool: but while I am coming, another steppeth down before me. Jesus saith unto him, Rise, take up thy bed, and walk. And immediately the man was made whole, and took up his bed, and walked: and on the same day was the sabbath. The Jews therefore said unto him that was cured, It is the sabbath day: it is not lawful for thee to carry thy bed. He answered them, He that made me whole, the same said unto me, Take up thy bed, and walk. Then asked they him, What man is that which said unto thee, Take up thy bed, and walk? And he that was healed wist not who it was: for Jesus had conveyed himself away, a multitude being in that place. Afterward Jesus findeth him in the temple, and said unto him, Behold, thou art made whole: sin no more, lest a worse thing come unto thee. The man departed, and told the Jews that it was Jesus, which had made him whole. And therefore did the Jews persecute Jesus, and sought to slay him, because he had done these things on the sabbath day."

(John 5:1–16)

Man accused God of wrongdoing because Jesus performed miracles on the Sabbath. This lame man had no way of getting down to the pool when the water was stirred, and the first one down to the pool was made whole. There was no one to help him down, and by the time he reached the pool on his own, someone else had beat him to the punch. Jesus didn't waste any time. He told him to take up his bed and walk. Immediately the man was made whole. Jesus bypassed the pool and went straight to the healing of this man's disease.

The Jews immediately asked the man what had happened in that moment. They approached him with a critical spirit and asked him, "Is it lawful for you to carry your bed on the Sabbath?" The man answered and told them that a man he did not know had healed him. Of course, the legalistic criticizers of Jesus were not going to let this one go. Jesus removed himself from the area because He anticipated the trouble. Jesus knew the heart of this man and that he had in all probability come from a troubled past. Jesus fixed this man's legs and his heart at the same time. However, God is not a puppeteer. He allows us to exercise the ability to choose our course, so Jesus told him to go and sin no more or a worse thing would come upon him.

The healed man was excited about his ability to walk, and after Jesus identified himself and gave him the instruction, he immediately proceeded to the critical Jews and told them it was Jesus who had healed him. In this instant we do not see any thanks, praise, or offering of a life in complete surrender. What we do see is a tattle-tale in action, a heart not thinking of the bigger picture and the counsel that Jesus gave. He was healed from the crippling disease of sin. Was he going to give in to the trap of sin again? This was the very thing that Jesus warned against. We do not know the final outcome of this man's experience. However, the lesson we can learn is that the human heart needs constant reminders of potential dangers that lead to the trappings of sin. Thank God when His healing promise is granted to you. Demonstrate wisdom with your day-to-day living. When God works a miracle in an individual, He gives the option of choosing a better way for the remainder of one's days on this planet. It is disappointing to God and it breaks His heart when we fail to exercise what we know is right. After this man told the Jews it was Jesus who healed him, they wanted to kill Him. When God puts His hand on us and raises us up, He intends the work to last. It is His purpose that we remain free of those things that cripple us. Stay free. Rise and walk, and do not take up the crippling thing again or something worse can happen to you.

Jesus Heals the Blind Man

> *"And as Jesus passed by, he saw a man which was blind from his birth. And his disciples asked him, saying, Master, who did sin, this*

man, or his parents, that he was born blind? Jesus answered, Nei-
ther hath this man sinned, nor his parents: but that the works of
God should be made manifest in him. I must work the works of him
that sent me, while it is day: the night cometh, when no man can
work. As long as I am in the world, I am the light of the world.
When he had thus spoken, he spat on the ground, and made clay of
the spittle, and he anointed the eyes of the blind man with the clay,
And said unto him, Go, wash in the pool of Siloam, (which is by
interpretation, Sent.) He went his way therefore, and washed, and
came seeing."

(John 9:1–7)

In this miracle Jesus made it very clear that neither the man nor his parents were guilty of sin. Most of the disciples were familiar with traditions that named sin as the cause for chronic illness or physical malady from birth. In the case of Job, as you read the account in detail, you will discover his three supposed friends accused him of this. By contrast, it is not always sin that causes the suffering. There are good people who suffer every day from the careless acts of others. What you choose to do with your life doesn't just affect you; it affects your world and the people close to you. In the case of this blind man, he did not sin. God had a special purpose in this suffering, to manifest His omnipotent power. This healing was provided by His strong compassionate love. It was done to prove to the world that there aren't boundaries or walls that God has constructed. There is definite purpose for sickness, and sin can be a cause for sickness. However, God always reveals His purpose in all suffering whether it is for His glory and praise, correction, and reproof or for meeting our Savior in glory. If there are any walls built, they are strictly our own. Jesus assured the disciples that it was not sin at all. He said that the works of God needed to be seen and that He was the light of the world. The blind man saw the light of God, and this light of God permeated his whole being. Not only were the eyes of this man physically opened, the light of his soul and spirit was illuminated to all of God. The only cure for spiritual blindness comes from Jesus. This is an example of a miracle worked by God solely for the purpose of convincing man of His power to do anything. Nothing is impossible with God.

Jesus Heals the Demon-possessed Man

"Then was brought unto him one possessed with a devil, blind, and dumb: and he healed him, insomuch that the blind and dumb both spake and saw. And all the people were amazed, and said, Is not this the son of David? But when the Pharisees heard it, they said, This fellow doth not cast out devils, but by Beelzebubb the prince of the devils. And Jesus knew their thoughts, and said unto them, Every kingdom divided against itself is brought to desolation; and every city or house divided against itself shall not stand: And if Satan cast out Satan, he is divided against himself; how shall then his kingdom stand? And if I by Beelzebub cast out devils, by whom do your children cast them out? therefore they shall be your judges. But if I cast out devils by the Spirit of God, then the kingdom of God is come unto you. Or else how can one enter into a strong man's house, and spoil his goods, except he first bind the strong man? and then he will spoil his house. He that is not with me is against me; and he that gathereth not with me scattereth abroad. Wherefore I say unto you, All manner of sin and blasphemy shall be forgiven unto men: but the blasphemy against the Holy Ghost shall not be forgiven unto men. And whosoever speaketh a word against the Son of man, it shall be forgiven him: but whosoever speaketh against the Holy Ghost, it shall not be forgiven him, neither in this world, neither in the world to come. Either make the tree good, and his fruit good; or else make the tree corrupt, and his fruit corrupt: for the tree is known by his fruit. O generation of vipers, how can ye, being evil, speak good things? for out of the abundance of the heart the mouth speaketh. A good man out of the good treasure of the heart bringeth forth good things: and an evil man out of the evil treasure bringeth forth evil things. But I say unto you, That every idle word that men shall speak, they shall give account thereof in the day of judgment. For by thy words thou shalt be justified, and by thy words thou shalt be condemned"

(Matthew 12:22–37)

This healing confounded the religious thinkers of the day. A man was brought to Jesus who was devil possessed, blind, and dumb. This is exactly the plan of Satan—for one to remain possessed, blind, and dumb. Imagine not seeing anything, being unable to speak, and the master manipulator confounds, confines, and deceives, keeping the shackles on for as long as possible. What a terrible life! Jesus set this man free instantly. Jesus healed him and was immediately accused of being a devil himself. Jesus knew the thoughts of the religious leaders of the day and told them that a kingdom divided would not stand, and that evil cannot heal evil. This miracle was performed to demonstrate the darkened and narrowed state of these great religious thinkers and to demonstrate the power of God over all darkness. Jesus revealed the true intent of the hearts of these religious people and rebuked it strongly. His healing power broke the chains of darkness and set this captive free.

This healing account teaches us several things:

1. The curse and darkness is broken by God and by His power. Only God has the power to rebuke evil. In our own strength and in our own name we haven't any power over Satan. It is by the power of the Lord Jesus and His cleansing blood that evil is broken and a freeway to eternal life is built.
2. The power of God is affirmed strongly, and though the great thinkers of the day were disputing it, they remained convicted because Jesus addressed the heart of the issue. They could not debate the matter.
3. The healing work of God confounds the intelligent. God blesses us with intellect, but He communicates to us through the spirit. The mind deduces and decides what the spirit has received from God. Our choices and actions result from that movement of God, or at least they should. In the case of the Pharisees, it moved them to further rebellion, be-

cause they refused to accept the truth about the corruption of their own hearts and the need for a complete change of heart and mind.

4. Good things proceed out of surrendered hearts. Jesus told the Pharisees that out of the abundance of the heart the mouth will speak. If the heart is dark, dark things proceed. When the heart is pure, good things proceed out of life.

5. Finally, the greatest lesson of all is that idle words deal a crushing blow. On the day of judgment every idle word will be accounted for. It seems that God hates idleness in any form, whether in word or action. We should all purpose to keep our hearts free from idle talk and actions. Our natural human tendency is to speak before thinking. We get to the point where we wish we had not said some careless thing, but it's too late to take it back. Be careful! When you write an email to someone about a sensitive issue, think twice before you hit the send button. It is too late to take it back when a mistake is made. I remember receiving an email from someone who did not intend the message to come to me at all. When I received the message it had my name on it, but it was intended for someone else. The email was full of negative communication about another person I knew. This person was the subject of serious criticism, and the email was not addressed to this individual. I was disturbed after receiving this email and prayed that God would help the sender to develop love and understanding. It has been said that idleness is the devil's workshop, and it is. God instructs that we will be justified by our words or convicted by our words. Let's purpose to be free from regret and speak the best before God and our neighbors. And be careful of those stray emails.

Ten Lepers and Only One Thanked Him

"And it came to pass, as he went to Jerusalem, that he passed through the midst of Samaria and Galilee. And as he entered into a certain village, there met him ten men that were lepers, which stood afar off: And they lifted up their voices, and said, Jesus, Master, have mercy on us. And when he saw them, he said unto them, Go shew yourselves unto the priests. And it came to pass, that, as they went, they were cleansed. And one of them, when he saw that he was healed, turned back, and with a loud voice glorified God, And fell down on his face at his feet, giving him thanks: and he was a Samaritan. And Jesus answering said, Were there not ten cleansed? but where are the nine? There are not found that returned to give glory to God, save this stranger. And he said unto him, Arise, go thy way: thy faith hath made thee whole."

(Luke 17:11–19)

The lesson of thankfulness and the necessity of it are illustrated in this healing account. Jesus healed ten men in need; all experienced the same malady. All had the same reasons to offer thanks to God, but only one did. It is within our nature to forget quickly. The Bible clearly illustrates this human deficiency and outlines the cost of such thanklessness. Only one turned back and gave glory to God. Only one had enough faith to recognize the miraculous work of God. A Samaritan thanked the Master. Samaritans were not liked by the religious Jews of the day. They were considered half-breeds, not entitled to the same benefits as a fullblooded Jew. They were considered unclean. Jesus told this story to demonstrate that there is no prejudice that can obstruct the just working of God. His own people were thankless and so the faith of this Samaritan was justified and praised. In my own work as a physician I have had many opportunities administering care to individuals who are the less fortunate. I have observed a greater receptivity to God and more thankfulness than I see in professing Christians.

When we cry out to the Master in desperation, we should also cry out in praise for what God has done! Jesus affirmed this man's faith. Not because He returned, but because he recognized the work of God. He recognized the source and power of his healing. His heart waited in expectation and received. This is a good example for us today. We ask of God, we wait with expectation for His work, we receive from Him, and then we praise Him for what He has done. The other nine may have left with a physical healing of the lesions of leprosy, but their souls and spirits contained a form of leprosy that had no physical remedy. Jesus clearly recognized their heart leprosy. Why do you want Jesus to heal you? If it is for the same motivations as the nine, which most likely was out of desperation as demonstrated by their thanklessness, you're heading for trouble!

Jesus Heals the Ear of a Defender

"And one of them smote the servant of the high priest, and cut off his right ear. And Jesus answered and said, Suffer ye thus far. And he touched his ear, and healed him."

(Luke 22:50–51)

Even during the most distressing time of Jesus' ministry, He healed. A defender was aware of the injustice of the accusations and charges placed upon Jesus. In Luke this man that came to the defense of Jesus is not named; however, in John 18 the man is identified as Peter.

Then Simon Peter having a sword drew it, and smote the high priest's servant, and cut off his right ear. The servant's name was Malchus. Then said Jesus unto Peter, Put up thy sword into the sheath: the cup which my Father hath given me, shall I not drink it?

(John 18:10–11)

This was a courageous act of defense but one that was quickly taken care of by complete restoring of Malchus's ear, as recorded in Luke. Jesus dumbfounded them all. What does this demonstrate? Quite a few lessons can be learned from this experience.

1. **The will of God:** Jesus knew that the Father's will was to endure suffering to demonstrate obedience and submission to His design.

2. **The forgiveness and love of God:** This is a perfect example of loving those not easily loved. Who are the unforgiving and unlovable? Accusers, liars, manipulators, the unfair, those who are unjust, and the ungodly. Forgiving those who love you is easy. Forgiving the unlovable, the mean, and the brutish is hard. Jesus did it to demonstrate that we can do it.

3. **Enduring suffering with no defense from men:** This is one of the toughest lessons of life. We want someone to help us and present our case. Jesus was nailed to the cross, rejected with no hope of human justice, but with the understanding of God's purpose and plan. This is too hard for us to do in our own humanity. There are no volunteers for such an experience. Job did not volunteer—he was selected. We may be selected and, if we are, God will meet us with grace; we will develop grit to stick to the task assigned. Just as He met the Apostle Paul with grace, direction, and power in his numerous experiences of being shipwrecked, imprisoned, and beaten for Jesus his Lord! Through the process of his ministry he developed the grit, grace, obedience, and perseverance—the marks of a Christian. He will meet you in times of suffering and bestow the same grit to go through victoriously! Spend some time studying the Acts of the Apostles and catch the spirit and vastness of the mission

and calling of His disciples and the power for service that was given to them for the evangelizing message of forgiveness of sin and the victorious message of eternal life in Christ, the redeemer of all.

4. **Mission of God:** The greatest lesson extracted from this experience is the mission of God. The need to obey His will, forgive and love enemies, endure suffering and shame with no human defense was all in the mission. God gives courage, grace, mercy, wisdom, comfort, and defense for the mission. All of these are demonstrated at the appropriate time and place. When Jesus proclaimed that it was finished, He meant that His full and total commitment to the mission of the Father God was complete. God accepted His Son, though His body was bruised for our transgressions, with open loving arms, placing Him at the right hand of the throne of God. This prominent place was saved for Him because He endured the suffering and the shame of it. God will grant us a place of prominence; it all hinges upon the completion of our mission and purpose designed by God for us to fulfill in this life.

One that Jesus Loved Raised from the Dead

"Now a certain man was sick, named Lazarus, of Bethany, the town of Mary and her sister Martha. (It was that Mary which anointed the Lord with ointment, and wiped his feet with her hair, whose brother Lazarus was sick). Therefore his sisters sent unto him, saying, Lord, behold, he whom thou lovest is sick. When Jesus heard that, he said, This sickness is not unto death, but for the glory of God, that the Son of God might be glorified thereby. Now Jesus loved Martha, and her sister, and Lazarus. When he had heard therefore that he was sick, he abode two days still in the same place where he was. Then after that saith he to his disciples, Let us go into Judaea again. His disciples say unto him, Master, the Jews of late sought to

stone thee; and goest thou thither again? Jesus answered, Are there not twelve hours in the day? If any man walk in the day, he stumbleth not, because he seeth the light of this world. But if a man walk in the night, he stumbleth, because there is no light in him. These things said he: and after that he saith unto them, Our friend Lazarus sleepeth; but I go, that I may awake him out of sleep. Then said his disciples, Lord, if he sleep, he shall do well. Howbeit Jesus spake of his death: but they thought that he had spoken of taking of rest in sleep. Then said Jesus unto them plainly, Lazarus is dead. And I am glad for your sakes that I was not there, to the intent ye may believe; nevertheless let us go unto him. Then said Thomas, which is called Didymus, unto his fellow disciples, Let us also go, that we may die with him. Then when Jesus came, he found that he had lain in the grave four days already. Now Bethany was nigh unto Jerusalem, about fifteen furlongs off: And many of the Jews came to Martha and Mary, to comfort them concerning their brother. Then Martha, as soon as she heard that Jesus was coming, went and met him: but Mary sat still in the house. Then said Martha unto Jesus, Lord, if thou hadst been here, my brother had not died. But I know, that even now, whatsoever thou wilt ask of God, God will give it thee. Jesus saith unto her, Thy brother shall rise again. Martha saith unto him, I know that he shall rise again in the resurrection at the last day. Jesus said unto her, I am the resurrection, and the life: he that believeth in me, though he were dead, yet shall he live: And whosoever liveth and believeth in me shall never die. Believest thou this? She saith unto him, Yea, Lord: I believe that thou art the Christ, the Son of God, which should come into the world. And when she had so said, she went her way, and called Mary her sister secretly, saying, The Master is come, and calleth for thee. As soon as she heard that, she arose quickly, and came unto him. Now Jesus was not yet come into the town, but was in that place where Martha met him. The Jews then which were with her in the house, and comforted her, when they saw Mary, that she rose up hastily and went out, followed her, saying, She goeth unto the grave to weep there. Then when Mary was come where Jesus was, and saw him, she fell down at his feet, saying unto him, Lord, if thou hadst been here, my brother had not died. When Jesus therefore saw her weeping, and the Jews also weeping which came with her, he groaned in the spirit, and was troubled, And said, Where have ye laid him? They said unto him,

Lord, come and see. Jesus wept. Then said the Jews, Behold how he
loved him! And some of them said, Could not this man, which opened
the eyes of the blind, have caused that even this man should not
have died? Jesus therefore again groaning in himself cometh to the
grave. It was a cave, and a stone lay upon it. Jesus said, Take ye
away the stone. Martha, the sister of him that was dead, saith unto
him, Lord, by this time he stinketh: for he hath been dead four days.
Jesus saith unto her, Said I not unto thee, that, if thou wouldest
believe, thou shouldest see the glory of God? Then they took away
the stone from the place where the dead was laid. And Jesus lifted
up his eyes, and said, Father, I thank thee that thou hast heard me.
And I knew that thou hearest me always: but because of the people
which stand by I said it, that they may believe that thou hast sent
me. And when he thus had spoken, he cried with a loud voice,
Lazarus, come forth. And he that was dead came forth, bound hand
and foot with grave clothes: and his face was bound about with a
napkin. Jesus saith unto them, Loose him, and let him go."
(John 11:1–44)

We clearly see a touching account of love, loss, grief, compassion, faith, expectation, and fulfillment. Jesus lost more than just a friend; He lost one as close as a brother. Jesus wept. These two words describe the human emotion expressed from His heart of love; He grieved the loss like the rest of the family. The day that God cried is recorded for us to see through the ages. This God cried tears just like us when touched by the human emotion of grief and sadness.

Jesus did not allow the human emotion of grief and sadness to obscure His mission of bringing Lazarus back to life. This was a miracle that He fully expected to perform in the power and name of His Father. Jesus prayed and thanked God for the work He was going to perform (faith in action). A cementing of His mission was manifested toward the loved ones grieving over Lazarus. Jesus shouted for Lazarus to come out; and he came out. A once-dead man clothed in grave clothes, with his face bound by a burial napkin, came forth. He wasn't a pale, gray, dead man any longer; he was pink, alive, and happy, excited to see his Master and friend. Jesus prepared the family members and friends and instructed them to go up to him and take off the grave clothes and let him go. I can picture it. Their mouths hung open in amazement and perplexity. Jesus healed and raised Lazarus. Never in their human experiences had they seen anything like this! The miracle of a life restored from the finiteness of death. A miracle of God performed by the hands of His Son for all generations to read and know. This fulfillment of a life restored is available for you. God always keeps His promises, and your life can be safely placed in His hands. As He raised Lazarus to life, so will He raise you up.

CHAPTER TEN

Healing, Brokenness, and Maturity

Being broken is a very systematic process from God's point of view. We see only the chaos of brokenness—we feel the pain, confusion and disorientation. God, however, doesn't react to life's circumstances. He is fully aware of what is happening to us even before it happens . . . . God never loses control of the breaking process.

(Dr. Charles Stanley)

Have you ever wondered why God allows us to suffer hard times? God allows us to experience hard times for the purpose of drawing us closer to Him, depending upon Him for everything, lifting every burden in prayer, allowing Him to be in full control, and accepting His teaching that can lead us to maturity in the spirit.

Brokenness is the process that God works through to accomplish this great work. God always has the finished product in view and never loses confidence that His children will make it through. Think of Daniel and his three faithful friends when they were delivered to the King and falsely accused and forced to face punishment for worshipping their God. The King meant to break them of this dependence upon God for everything and commanded their complete devotion and worship. God, on the other hand, meant it to demonstrate their faith and devotion to Him. This was a breaking process within God's control for a new dimension of faith and trust demonstrated to the King and his kingdom. I'm sure that Daniel and his three devoted friends knew in their hearts that God would keep and deliver them. However, there is always the process and I'm sure that they were not aware of the full plan of God in this situation. This is also part of the process of brokenness, maybe on a different level, but brokenness nonetheless.

When we initially come to God and ask Him to forgive us of our sin and accept his free gift of salvation, this is a breaking process. God has blessed us with free will, and He allows us to decide whether to give it all to Him or rebel against Him. The anguish of heart experienced when we choose to live without God is the beginning of the breaking process that either leads to acceptance that God is in control of everything or a rejection of His complete control. When God is ruling supreme in your life and you suffer a sickness of some kind and wait for His healing, the process is one of brokenness. God's pleasure is in a broken and devoted heart. To be broken is painful and difficult, but needful. The process happens by degrees over the course of life, not just in an instant of time.

I remember being broken over my spiritual condition before I accepted Jesus into my life. When I accepted His forgiveness and love and asked Him to forgive my sin and my lack of love toward Him, the burden of my dark life lifted and a new life began. The breaking process did not stop here. It was the beginning of a series of breaking experiences that were necessary to develop a closer reliance upon God. I know that it will continue until I meet Him in heaven. Do I understand all of it? No. Do I look forward to the next breaking experience? Let's just say that God knows what He is doing whether I understand it or not. I do not believe anyone says happily that they're so glad that God is going to tear their world apart and put the pieces back in better order than ever before. Personally, I like the second part of the sentence. But I do realize that it would not happen if I did not experience the breaking process. The joy of the Lord should be our strength. What can take us through this breaking and growing process? The joy of the Lord will take us through. I may not be joyful about the process of reaching brokenness, but I am joyful because I know that God is in charge and that He will see me through. Blessing and brokenness go together, and I know that this is hard to comprehend in human terms. The ultimate purpose of the process is to develop a greater maturity in Him. When we respond in faith, each test and affliction teaches a greater dimension of His love and stronger reliance upon His promises.

God knows what is needed to develop total reliance upon Him, and He targets that area. The enemy knows our weaknesses and targets these areas in hopes we will give in to his temptations. God is in control regardless. The adversary is not going to tempt the servant with the same temptation of the queen and vice versa. The temptations of the adversary and his forces are fitting for the individual weaknesses to keep one in bondage and eternal ruin. This was the purpose in Job's suffering. But the bottom line is that God was and is in control. God ordains the breaking process for growth and maturity.

When we are experiencing brokenness, the process will affect others in our world. Joseph was a prime example of this when his brothers sold him into Egyptian slavery. They thought they would be rid of this spoiled-brat dreamer for good. This was the beginning of their breaking process—and a long one, too. It was also the beginning of Joseph's breaking process for the greater plan of God to be accomplished. What Joseph's brothers meant for harm, God meant for good, further demonstrating that God was in control. The result of the long, arduous journey was total dependence upon God, forgiveness, leadership, perfect love, acceptance, and ultimately the will of God. Healing depends upon our willingness to be broken for God and our desire to grow and mature in faith. Complete healing results when we submit our all and become more like the Master in our attitudes, habits, and actions. Can God heal without using the process? God can do anything at any time. However, most accounts that I have read in the Bible and in shared experiences of others demonstrate the realization of a specific need. This realization is a process, and when the time is right God heals either miraculously or through the process of time. In some cases He chooses to remain silent—as in the case of the Apostle Paul— for a specific reason that will be revealed only in eternity. God wants to heal you, but it may not be in the way you are expecting. You may need healing in areas of your life that you are not aware of. Leave it to Him. He is in charge and in complete control. All you need to do is realize this providential fact: The things that are humanly impossible are Divinely possible.

CHAPTER ELEVEN

Jesus Heals Me!

"My child, allow me to do what I will with you. I know what is best for you. You think as a man; you feel in many things as human affection persuades."[17]

"Every fiber of my soul was tingling with a sense of God's presence."

(A. B. Simpson)

Settling the Matter with God

There comes a time in our walk with God when we must stop putting God's will against our own will and give in to the divine plan. A good illustration of aligning with the will of God is the story of Jacob in Genesis 32: 22–32. Jacob submitted to God's overtures and stopped his fighting with God. Jacob, after giving in to God's plan, received the greatest blessing, the heritage of God promised to all succeeding generations! A.B. Simpson talks about settling the matter with God in his personal testimony of healing.

In the summer I speak of, I heard a great number of people testify that they had been healed by simply trusting the Word of Christ, just as they would for their salvation. These testimonies drove me to my Bible. I determined that I must settle the matter one way or the other. I am glad I did not go to man. At Jesus' feet, alone, with my Bible open and with no one to help or guide me, I became convinced that this was part of Christ's glorious gospel for a sinful and suffering world—the purchase of His blessed cross for all who would believe and receive His Word.[18]

At the feet of Jesus is where we are to lay it all. Every need that we have can be placed there. This may sound old fashioned, but it is the truth. There is no way around it. Healing happens at the feet of Jesus.

Your Faith Has Made You Complete

"Your faith has made you whole," was the reply of Jesus. I often hear, "I have been waiting a long time and I don't believe that God is going to heal me." I hear this from individuals who have been worn down by sickness, sadness, and constant affliction. It is so important to wait expectantly and not be given to disappointment and disillusionment. As we've seen, a blind man suffered for many years, a woman lived with a chronic bleeding disorder and couldn't find help from the physicians of the day, a lame man waited for years before he walked, Elijah was set aside at the brook for his experience of healing and restoration. And we may be required to wait for God's timing for healing.

Can Jesus heal me? Or even, *will* Jesus heal me? More appropriately, *when* Jesus heals me, my heart will rejoice. But until then I will wait with a spirit of expectancy like so many biblical examples and great heroes of faith did through the ages. The Apostle Paul sought God for healing on many occasions and didn't get a firm answer. Yet he was filled with the presence of the Holy Spirit to achieve great things. His spirit of expectancy and submission to God provided the greatest writings of the New Testament inspired by the presence of God in his life.

You have work to do. Work that God is requiring you to do. Don't put your life on hold. Don't just wait for your healing. Work for the Lord in a spirit of expectancy and faith until He grants you the miracle. The time will be well spent, and, like Paul, you can exclaim that His strength is made perfect in your weaknesses. If it is not God's will to heal you, then your service to Him will prove to be, as in the case of Paul, an effective and hopeful ministry. Paul did not give up. You must not give up.

Don't accept any counterfeit offers that may heal the physical temporarily and vex the soul and spirit. It is easy when you are vulnerable and desperate to grasp at anything that offers any glimmer of healing. There are many dangerous and false healing methods that exist in the world; unfortunately there are many so-called Christian healers who are just as dangerous. Throughout this entire work you have heard me say that healing is from God and God alone. He can use any means, and if He chooses to work through a doctor, minister, friend, or process, you will know it is from God because the experience brings peace, harmony, firm assurance, and a lasting hope. The key is that your faith and trust are in Him, your patience is in Him, your expectancy is in Him, your hope is in Him, and you are growing into an unwavering, living faith. Job said, "Though he slay me, yet will I trust Him." Remember, you are His holy temple created in His image, an imprint in the palm of His hand, and all is within His control and timing.

Loving Jesus Above All Things

Your very first priority in order to receive the blessing of healing is to love Jesus above all. You have probably read this many times throughout this book. You can also read this in the Bible, in any work authored by a faithful follower of Christ, in any life that demonstrates active faith and trust in Christ, and in any saint of God who determines to love the Master!

Maybe you are the saint with a healing experience to share. Have you received the touch of the Master? Let me tell you about a wonderful woman who came to see me about five years ago. When Tammy arrived at the clinic where I practice medicine she had been diagnosed with breast cancer that had spread to her spine and lungs. She was very ill. Her frame was fragile, and she was stick thin with gray, pale skin. She was carried into the clinic by her husband because she was too weak to walk. This woman and her husband came from several generations of Jehovah's Witnesses and failed to see the power of God in healing, though they prayed and followed to the letter all the requirements to satisfy their religious experience. The first words out of this lovely woman's mouth were; "Dr. John, is there hope for me?" In the first place, there is hope for all who call on the name of the Lord in desperate situations when the desire is to experience the fullness of God's healing.

The most essential need here was establishing trust, as she had already been to many doctors and was let down by them in one way or another. Another need was to help her to conquer fear, which seemed to have a firm grip on her. During the first visit we discussed her options for treatment, and she was willing to do whatever was necessary to get well. We could not discuss particulars regarding spiritual health at this time. This was virtually a closed door confirmed by the fact that when I asked her if she wanted to pray for healing she immediately resisted and said no. Part of winning her trust was to not force the issue, though I knew that my prayers would be lifted up for her to God for her healing in the areas that mattered most.

After two months of treatment, an amazing transformation occurred. She began to gain weight, her breast sores began to heal, her skin color returned to a pink tone, and life was back in her face. The Holy Spirit was healing her on the inside, demonstrating His power, and her physical body was manifesting the results. During this time she proceeded to let me know that the reason she didn't want me to pray for her was because she was struggling with the fact that God had not heard her prayers in the past even though she memorized large passages of scripture and did all the things required to be a good Jehovah's Witness. Her position was that if God didn't hear her then, He certainly wasn't going to hear her now. I assured her that the God of the Bible, through a personal faith in Jesus Christ, was different than what she had experienced previously. After confirming this, she asked me to pray with her. We prayed together with her husband also present and asked God to manifest himself through Tammy by healing every wounded place. Tammy's tears flowed because she was already experiencing the touch of God in a way she had never experienced. She accepted Jesus as her Savior by personal faith. Her husband also accepted Jesus. Both immediately made a complete break from the longstanding tradition of religious bondage. Immediately, Tammy and her husband encountered rejection from family members and supposed friends. Their entire world changed, and God gave the grace to meet the trial. Tammy is still living today—five years from the first time I saw her. She still battles cancer. She wrote me a long note thanking God and her doctor for the life extension and for being able to celebrate her 25th wedding anniversary and for the gift of raising her daughter who is now 18 years old and past the turbulent years. She exclaimed; "I am celebrating life, and Jesus has made it possible." I say thank God for knowing the parts of us that need His touch.

The following excerpt says it well:

"BLESSED is he who appreciates what it is to love Jesus and who despises himself for the sake of Jesus. Give up all other love for His, since He wishes to be loved alone above all things. Affection for creatures is deceitful and inconstant, but the love of Jesus is true and enduring. He who clings to a creature will fall with its frailty, but he who gives himself to Jesus will ever be strengthened. Love Him, then; keep Him as a friend. He will not leave you as others do, or let you suffer lasting death. Sometime, whether you will or not, you will have to part with everything. Cling, therefore, to Jesus in life and death; trust yourself to the glory of Him who alone can help you when all others fail. Your Beloved is such that He will not accept what belongs to another—He wants your heart for himself alone, to be enthroned therein as King in His own right. If you but knew how to free yourself entirely from all creatures, Jesus would gladly dwell within you. You will find, apart from Him, that nearly all the trust you place in men is a total loss. Therefore, neither confide in nor depend upon a wind-shaken reed, for "all flesh is grass" and all its glory, like the flower of grass, will fade away. You will quickly be deceived if you look only to the outward appearance of men, and you will often be disappointed if you seek comfort and gain in them. If, however, you seek Jesus in all things, you will surely find Him. Likewise, if you seek yourself, you will find yourself—to your own ruin. For the man who does not seek Jesus does himself much greater harm than the whole world and all his enemies could ever do."[19]

Essential Points to Ponder

The essentials of the healing journey contain the following ingredients to assure a living commitment to God's design for your life. Healing and mystery walk side by side. Healing cannot always be explained in human terms, and the delay of healing cannot always be understood. When the miracle of healing happens, it is a surprise, and the grateful heart rejoices and gives praise to the Miracle Worker. The work is not on our timetable, and it is not brought in ways we plan or expect. It is in the impossibilities that God brings forth His best work. Think of all the impossible events that may have occurred in your life. Do you believe for one second that you did it all yourself? That is impossible. With God all things are possible!

- **Surrender**

  Complete surrender to the will and plan of God is essential. A surrendered life leads to a satisfied life. William Booth has said, "If we do not surrender to Christ we surrender to chaos." The way of the Lord is a refuge and shelter in times of trouble. Surrendering to Him is not giving up just because we have failed and have nowhere else to turn. Surrender is giving in to God's best plan for life. Life may throw challenges at us in ways we never expected. However, being safe in the arms of Jesus is where healing takes place. Surrendering is not giving up. It is giving in to the will and purpose of the Master, the safest place in the world to be.

- **Obedience**

  Consistent obedience is the result of complete surrender. We do not obey because we want to adhere to the rules for the rule's sake. It is an act of service to God to obey. It is a required course, and there are no ways around it if our desire is to serve God completely. Shortcuts don't count. It's complete obedience to God's mission and purpose for your life or nothing at all. Scripture teaches that it is better to obey than to sacrifice. Thomas Kempis sums it well:

  > *"It is a very great thing to obey, to live under a superior and not to be one's own master, for it is much safer to be subject than it is to command. Many live in obedience more from necessity than from love. Such become discontented and dejected on the slightest pretext; they will never gain peace of mind unless they subject themselves wholeheartedly for the love of God."*[20]

- **Worship and Praise**

  John Wesley, in his own experience, describes worship as the only way to a state of complete happiness in spirit. Not knowing God personally often leads us to pursue our happiness in other areas. Without the adoration and personal worship of God by our daily service, there is no true happiness. The things of this world can fade away, friendships can sour, and pleasure lasts only for a season. The only lasting form of fulfillment and eternal happiness is in the worship of our living God.

  > *"That something is neither more nor less than the knowledge and love of God; without which no spirit can be happy either in heaven or earth. Permit me to recite my own experience, in confirmation of this: I distinctly remember, that, even in my childhood, even when I was at school, I have often said, "They say the life of a schoolboy is the happiest in the world; but I am sure I am not happy; for I am not content, and so cannot be happy." When I had lived a few years longer, being in the vigour of youth, a stranger to pain and sickness, and particularly to lowness of spirits; (which I do not remember to have felt one quarter of an hour since I was born;) having plenty of all things, in the midst of sensible and amiable friends who loved me, and I loved them; and being in the way of life which, of all others, suited my inclinations; still I was not happy. I wondered why I was not, and could not imagine what the reason was. The reason certainly was, I did not know God; the Source of present as well as eternal happiness. What is a clear proof that I was not then happy is, that, upon the coolest reflection, I knew not one week which I would have thought it worth while to have lived over again; taking it with every inward and outward sensation, without any variation at all."*[21]

144

- **Commitment for the Impossibilities**
  The word *impossible* suggests being incapable of being done, attained, fulfilled, or insuperably difficult. When we are conformed to the image of Christ, the impossibilities are possible because faith affirms that with God all things are possible.

  > When the love of God has been shed abroad in our hearts, we have to exhibit it in the strain of life; when we are saved and sanctified we are apt to think that there is no strain, but Paul speaks of the "tribulation" which "worketh patience." I mean by strain, not effort, but the possibility of going wrong as well as of going right. There is always a risk, for this reason, that God values our obedience to Him.[22]

  When the healing touch of God is needed, as in the case of the woman with the bleeding disorder, she took the risk, she had strain and stress, she exhibited patience and perseverance, she reached out in faith! This woman was committed to the fact that the impossible was made possible with God. Job is another demonstration that God achieves the impossible; that through his persistent confidence in God, the impossible was made possible. Jesus provides the impossible through the work of the Holy Spirit. The comforter proves the active and living work of God in every matter of life for those who receive the Holy Spirit.

- **Willingness to Suffer for Christ**
  Suffering is a tough pill to swallow for the Christian. Suffering for Christ is not the same as suffering for the world. The world hates the things of God and resists a pure spirit. Jesus suffered for the evil of the whole world when He brought it all to the cross. It was so heavy and dark that not even the Father could bear to look at it. God loves us so

much that He *gave* His Son and He saw the pain and suffering for the sins of all of mankind, and He *gave* anyway. Jesus suffered the shame of it all and it spells out one word, l-o-v-e.

The Apostle Paul is no stranger when it comes to the ministry of suffering. In 2 Corinthians 11:23–29, you will discover the intensity of Paul's suffering shared for the purpose of preparing the believer for the hard times. Previously in 2 Corinthians 6:3–10, Paul outlines the ministry of suffering in detail. You will notice as you read that even in suffering, joy, truth, and complete blessing coexist.

Oswald Chambers eloquently describes such suffering:

> To "suffer as a Christian" is not to be marked peculiar because of your views, or because you will not bend to conventionality; these things are not Christian, but ordinary human traits from which all men suffer irrespective of creed or religion or no religion. To "suffer as a Christian" is to suffer because there is an essential difference between you and the world which rouses the contempt of the world, and the disgust and hatred of the spirit that is in the world. To "suffer as a Christian" is to have no answer when the world's satire is turned on you, as it was turned on Jesus Christ when He hung upon the cross, when they turned His words into jest and jeer; they will do the same to you. He gave no answer, neither can you.[23]

> WHAT are you saying, My child? Think of My suffering and that of the saints, and cease complaining. You have not yet resisted to the shedding of blood. What you suffer is very little compared with the great things they suffered who were so strongly tempted, so severely troubled, so tried and tormented in many ways. Well may you remember, therefore, the very painful woes of others, that you may bear your own little ones the more easily. And if they do not seem so small to you, examine if perhaps your impatience is not the cause of their apparent greatness; and whether

they are great or small, try to bear them all patiently. The better you dispose yourself to suffer, the more wisely you act and the greater is the reward promised you. [24]

You may not be able to explain it or figure it all out. There are many types of suffering, and there are times while in the throes of suffering that we begin to heal and mend. *"Beloved, think it not strange concerning the fiery trial which is to try you, as though some strange thing happened unto you: But rejoice, inasmuch as ye are partakers of Christ's sufferings; that, when his glory shall be revealed, ye may be glad also with exceeding joy."* (1 Peter 4:12–13).

• **Thankfulness and Steadfastness**
Thankfulness and steadfastness are solid examples of faith in action. These are not given to extremes. They are constant and reliable. The Christian life should be metered by our thankfulness and steadfastness. There is a poem that states this well:

> *Self-reliant but not Self-sufficient*
> *Energetic but not Self-seeking*
> *Steadfast but not Stubborn*
> *Tactful but not Timid*
> *Serious but not Sullen*
> *Loyal but not Sectarian*
> *Unmovable but not Stationary*
> *Gentle but not Hypersensitive*
> *Tenderhearted but not Touchy*
> *Conscientious but not a Perfectionist*
> *Disciplined but not Demanding*
> *Generous but not Gullible*
> *Meek but not Weak*
> *Humorous but not Hilarious*
> *Friendly but not Familiar*
> *Holy but not Holier-than-thou*

Discerning but not Critical
Progressive but not Pretentious[25]

Thankfulness and steadfastness allow us to keep a constant focus on the One who makes everything possible. There are no assumptions or pretentious actions on God's part; all are designed to equip His children for a more reasonable service. The Apostle Paul demonstrates a spirit of thankfulness and steadfastness through the most difficult times when he tells us, *"Not that I speak in respect of want: for I have learned, in whatsoever state I am, therewith to be content. I know both how to be abased, and I know how to abound: everywhere and in all things I am instructed both to be full and to be hungry, both to abound and to suffer need. I can do all things through Christ which strengtheneth me"* (Philippians 4:11–13).

Setting Your Sails Toward Joy

One last item I want to address in addition to thankfulness and steadfastness is that an individual's joy can be complete regardless of the obstacles and challenges that everyday living produces. How can we have complete joy in this life? Proverbs 15:13 says, *"A joyful heart maketh a cheerful countenance."* We must recognize God as being in full control of everything that touches life. External factors do not determine or guarantee joy. Education and intelligence do not determine joy. Status and position do not determine joy. Confidence and trust in God are the only determining factors of joy. *"Regardless how severely the winds of adversity may blow, we set our sails toward joy."*[26]

We must affirm with the Apostle Paul that joy is a lifelong pursuit. This is the reason Chuck Swindoll refers to the Apostle Paul as "a man of grace and grit." Oh that we can become the same in whatever state we find ourselves. Our total well-being depends upon it. Our healing depends upon it. Our eternal existence with God depends upon it!

Do the Work and Rest in God

Countless times I have seen and heard people wanting God to heal them, but they are not committed to following through and giving themselves over to God and doing the work He expects. Expecting healing without the work required in faith and trust in Christ is selfish. The requirement is for an individual to change bad habits and attitudes, develop a greater dependence on the grace and will of God, and to serve others despite personal pain, allowing God to work His greater purpose through it. We must *do the work* or we forfeit the promise and blessing. I like A.B. Simpson's writing called *Abiding and Confiding*:

I am crucified with Jesus,
And He lives and dwells with me;
I have ceased from all my struggling,
'Tis no longer I, but He.
All my will is yielded to Him,
And His Spirit reigns within;
And His precious blood each moment
Keeps me cleansed and free from sin.
All my sickness I bring Him,
And He bears them all away;
All my fears and griefs I tell Him,
All my cares from day to day.
All my strength I draw from Jesus,
By His breath I live and move;
E'en His very mind He gives me,
And His faith, and life, and love.
For my words I take His wisdom,
For my works His Spirit's power;
For my ways His ceaseless presence
Guards and guides me every hour.
Of my heart, He is the portion,

Of my joy the boundless spring;
Saviour, Sanctifier, Healer,
Glorious Lord, and coming King.[27]

I hope you learned some valuable life applications in healing. I count it a privilege to serve God in the healing ministry. The ultimate purpose in healing is to find your mission and purpose in Christ and to begin to fulfill the great commission of making disciples in all nations. Jesus healed the sick and required service in return. If you desire to be healed, it is in the healing service of God that we find the greatest healing of all. Our maladies can be made well through the miraculous work of Jesus, but the greatest healing miracle of all is the death and resurrection of our Lord Jesus. He set us free from the chains of sin and death.

When we come to know Him, we are healed. When we love Him, we are healed. When we serve Him, we are healed. When we meet Him at heaven's gate, we are healed!

Endnotes

1 Spurgeon C. H., *On Prayer and Spiritual Warfare*, Whitaker House, 1998.

2 Scientific American Mind; *Fear Not*, pp. 62–69 Jan., 2004.

3 Chambers, O., *The Complete Works of Oswald Chambers*, Discovery House Publishing, 2000.

4 Bounds E.M., *On Prayer*, Whitaker House, 1997.

5 Chambers, O. 1999, 1936. *Christian Disciplines II* (electronic ed.). Marshall, Morgan & Scott: London.

6 Wesley, J., *Wesley's Works*, *Sermon on the Mount*, Beacon Hill Press, Reprinted 1979.

7 Osbeck, K. W. 1990. Amazing Grace: *366 Inspiring Hymn Stories for Daily Devotions*. p. 353. Kregel Publications: Grand Rapids, Mich.

8 Chambers, O. 1996, 1960. *Studies in the Sermon on the Mount*. Marshall, Morgan & Scott: Hants, UK.

9 Keller, P., What Makes Life Worth Living; *Knowing God First-hand*, Nelson, 1998.

10 Schaeffer, Francis., *The Complete Works Of Francis A. Schaeffer; A Christian Worldview.* 1982, Vol. 5, p. 384.

11 Brand. P., Yancey. P., *Fearfully and Wonderfully Made*, Zondervan. 1980.

12 Schaeffer. F., *A Christian View of the West.* Volume 5; *How Should We Then Live?* 1982.

13 Kempis. T., *The Imitation of Christ.* Logos Research Systems: Oak Harbor, WA. 1996.

14 Ridley. M., *Nature Via Nurture*, HarperCollins, 2003.

15 Cialdini. R., Scientific American Mind; *The Science of Persuasion*, pp 70–77, Jan 2004.

16 Brand. P., Yancey. P., *Fearfully and Wonderfully Made.* Zondervan. 1980.

17 Kempis, T., *The Imitation of Christ*, Logos Research Systems: Oak Harbor, WA 1996.

18 Simpson, A, B., *The Gospel of Healing*, Christian Publications, Inc. 1994.

19 Kempis. T., *The Imitation of Christ.* Logos Research Systems: Oak Harbor, WA. 1996.

20 Kempis. T., *The Imitation of Christ.* Logos Research Systems: Oak Harbor, WA 1996.

21 Wesley, J., *Sermons, on Several Occasions.* Logos Research Systems, Inc.: Oak Harbor, WA, 1999.

22 Chambers, O., *Conformed to His Image*, Marshall, Morgan & Scott: London, 1996, 1950.

23 Chambers, O., *Christian Disciplines I,* (electronic ed.) Marshall, Morgan & Scott: London. 1999, 1936.

24 Kempis. T., *The Imitation of Christ* (Logos Research Systems: Oak Harbor, WA) 1996.

25 Tan, P. L., *Encyclopedia of 7700 Illustrations*, Bible Communications: Garland TX. 1996.

26 Swindoll, C., Wisdom For the Way, *Sails Set Toward Joy*, Thomas Nelson 2001.

27 Simpson, A.B., *The Gospel of Healing* (Christian Publications, Inc.) 1994.

To order additional copies of

Complete *by the*
Master's Touch

Have your credit card ready and call:
1-877-421-READ (7323)
or please visit our web site at
www.pleasantword.com
Also available at:
www.amazon.com
and
www.barnesandnoble.com

Other books by Dr. John A. Catanzaro:
Cancer an Integrative Approach
and forthcoming
Mapping Our Spiritual Genes

Printed in the United States
21926LVS00002B/481-534